T0123416

YOUR PET IS GONE

Life and Pet-Loss Coaching,
Growing from Grief to Greatness

DAN CRENSHAW

BALBOA.
PRESS

A DIVISION OF HAY HOUSE

Balboa Press books may be ordered through booksellers or by contacting:

Balboa Press
A Division of Hay House
1663 Liberty Drive
Bloomington, IN 47403
www.balboapress.com
1 (877) 407-4847

Because of the dynamic nature of the Internet, any web addresses or links contained in this book may have changed since publication and may no longer be valid. The views expressed in this work are solely those of the author and do not necessarily reflect the views of the publisher, and the publisher hereby disclaims any responsibility for them.

The author of this book does not dispense medical advice or prescribe the use of any technique as a form of treatment for physical, emotional, or medical problems without the advice of a physician, either directly or indirectly. The intent of the author is only to offer information of a general nature to help you in your quest for emotional and spiritual well-being. In the event you use any of the information in this book for yourself, which is your constitutional right, the author and the publisher assume no responsibility for your actions.

Any people depicted in stock imagery provided by Getty Images are models, and such images are being used for illustrative purposes only. Certain stock imagery © Getty Images.

Print information available on the last page.

ISBN: 978-1-9822-0452-5 (sc)
ISBN: 978-1-9822-0451-8 (e)

Balboa Press rev. date: 05/30/2018

CONTENTS

INTRODUCTION

May you experience Creative Furry Farewell Support,
As your grief-coping skills increase and your symptoms abort.

—*Dan Crenshaw*

T HIS BOOK CAN empower you to grow creatively through the grief of pet loss. First, through the arduous climb out of the valley of grief coping muscles can be strengthened. Second, it can guide you into using your enhanced coping skills to grow beyond grief to greatness. As a result, you can experience a transformation. While you are in the throes of grief, you may possibly not foresee a life after grief of greater excellence, purpose, and passion. This book can gradually enable you to obtain a lifestyle of purposeful positive action. Therefore this book is both life and pet loss coaching.

The level of anguish that many people experience when they lose a pet is often not understood. This book honors the pain that pet loss brings and demonstrates how creative grief work can result in gains. In bereavement, with dignity and reality, you can come to grips with death's finality.

Many people who have lost a pet can relate to the following poem that I wrote. This grief experience can begin right after grief's bolt of lightning has given you a jolt. This poem happens to be about the loss of a dog, but this book applies to the loss of any pet that can leave you in a dense fog.

When Your Dog is Gone

Dan C. Crenshaw

Doggone it, my dog is gone.
What went wrong?
Why can't I be strong?
People tell me tears do not belong.

These words throw salt on my bleeding heart.
It seems that my dog and I were never apart.
I need someone to understand.
The precious dog wagged his tail as I came home again and again.

"It was just a pet," I hear over and over.
He was more than a pet; he was my companion named Rover.
The look in his eyes let me know his love was mine.
He loved me 100 percent of the time.

In my mind, I heard melodious bells chime.
We relished each moment in harmony.
He never seemed angry with me.
He helped me to see what kind of person I could be.

My welcome home experiences will never be the same.
He always was elated when I came.
He danced and pranced in sheer delight.
No matter how the day went, my precious pet made things all right.

How can anyone say that his death was trite?
I loved that dog with all of my heart, soul, and might.
The bond that we had was out of sight.
Regarding life's values, he often helped me to see more light.

How much I miss him goes beyond words.
A painful memory constantly occurs.
Every moment we were together my heart was stirred.
Not taking this loss seriously is more than absurd.

I can see him romping in the fields in heaven waiting for me to come home.
Then we will feel each other's spirit as we playfully roam.
Doggone it, my dog is gone.
But I will see him when I go home.

Giving dignity instead of shame to your grief enables you to gain traction to begin the grief journey with appropriate action. You will need to give yourself compassion as you experience each painful intermittent reaction. Various coping muscles can be strengthened with grief work. Your healing can become a skillful journey as you forge through the valley of grief without becoming berserk.

Regarding grief, there is no deadline. No matter how long one lives, one generally does not completely cross the finish line. It is important that through the ups and downs you are moving forward bit by bit. Grief may leave some smaller emotional bruises, but you will not quit. You can manifest heroic grit. When these bruises surface, with dignified determination, you will keep your wit. You may have frustrations, each one will be a short-lived fit.

Grief can tax a person's emotions by its painful size. A heroic level of coping will need to arise. You will not listen to others' demeaning lies and what people ignorantly advise as you will seek allies. The enormous weight of grief can come as a shocking surprise. You will be able to live with the surfacing whys. You will know which coping skills to apply as you express your goodbyes, and let go resulting in grief's gradual demise.

As you adjust to the loss, you will improvise and not take your grief lightly or have it sensationalized. As a result, you will be able to allow the healing tears to pour from your eyes. You will have hope that out of the darkness the sun will rise. Your courage will end up giving you a renewed life prize. You can cut grief down to a manageable size as you set boundaries with people who encroach with unwise replies.

The pain of the loss of a pet can be from mild to monstrous. Some people may think a high level of pain is preposterous. In reality, pet loss can be like losing a significant other. People who do not understand pet loss may say, "Why bother?" Emotionally you may feel like you are your pet's mother or father. As a result, this priceless lost bond can feel like torture.

The bond may have seemed like a magic wand. This bond was worth more than a huge sparkling diamond. It seems that your tears could fill up a pond, but deep inside you know you can have a creative future. This loss can result in coping skills that spawn as your mourning becomes virtually gone.

Gradually the strangling, entangled emotions can become unraveled. You can begin another chapter of your life without feeling bedeviled. Then, your life will be less stressful, and you will become more zestful. Throughout the journey of grief, you will miss the bark. With courage, you will be ready for your grief journey's start.

A new beginning, will not feel as stark as your grief will not seem as dark. You are journeying toward grief's healing mark. When the pain of grief begins to fade, you will see new possibilities that can be made. You will not experience pet loss as an overwhelming pestilence. The second part of this book reveals how your enhanced coping skills can strengthen your life's excellence.

In effect, this book is broader than pet loss as it is a life-coaching book that grants purposeful lifestyle guidance. The book includes healing inspiration specific to coping with pet loss's stridence. This information can help you integrate pet loss coping skills into life as a whole. As a result, your coping skills can become more holistic.

Once I was playing the trumpet for people with developmental disabilities. I began to experience an inexplicable deep sense of peacefulness. I felt that I was at one with the trumpet, with the people in attendance, as well as deeply connected with myself and the world spiritually. The trumpet seemed to be playing itself. Something outside me seemed to be flowing through me. I felt a sense of connectedness with all that was around me. As I finished, a psychologist from the next room came in and said, "I do not know what it was about the music you played, but it impacted me deeply." It was one of those deeply peaceful experiences that had a powerful effect on me and the psychologist as well. The positive vibrations led to deeply felt rich

Sensations in which to peacefully dwell.

The intention of this book is to be realistic, and not overly simplistic. It has substance that can help you to become more hopeful and optimistic. It can h help you to accept your limitations and enhance your possibilities. You do not have to cover up your life's challenges. You do not have to say that difficulties are gone. You can move from grief to greatness as your grief subsides and ends in a song.

PART 1

CREATIVE SUPPORT WHEN YOUR PET IS GONE

CHAPTER 1

The Significance of Human-Animal Bond

The human-animal bond can seem like a magic wand.

—*Dan Crenshaw*

MANY WORDS CAN be used to describe the different aspects of human-animal bonding. For many people, this bond can help quench a life's deep longing. These relational jewels can result in experiencing many life renewals. One's pet can be like a playful child, loyal friend, pal, and wonderful companion. This remarkable relationship can be like experiencing the Grand Canyon. The pet bond can vastly increase your life's vistas. As a result, your pet can seem like the eighth wonder of the world, and your life can increasingly unfurl. Because your bond with your pet mattered losing your pet can feel like your heart is deeply tattered.

The nutrients of this relationship can provide emotional vitamins, which can result in a healthy, emotional high. This healthy feeling can help prevent sickness from coming nigh. The bond can become surreal, but it is the real deal. The contributions can engender a rewarding relationship that can become a thrill. Also, your pet can become consoling like a parent, and you naturally wish that this remarkable beneficial relationship would never end. It is hard to imagine that this contribution could be lost and feel like a deficit yearning to mend.

Years ago, I spoke to a senior citizen's group. One senior citizen had a special dog sitting at her feet. He helped her in a vital aspect of her life. The dog's special assistance enhanced the elderly person's quality of life. The relational bond and skillful help resulted in the dog becoming her life's highlight.

Once, I was running in my first 10 kilometers race at the Cooper River

Bridge Run in Charleston, South Carolina. As I stood in line waiting for the race to begin, next to me was a gentleman wearing a cap with a pigeon within. He took off his cap to reveal what he emotionally felt was his next of kin. He said that when this bird popped out of its egg's shell, their eyes met and bonding was soon to begin.

He said he used to allow the bird to fly above him in his races. Now, with thousands of people participating, he was concerned that his pigeon would lose sight of him in the midst of so many faces. Then I noticed a reporter with a TV camera emerge through the crowd. The local TV station had heard about this fascinating relationship between a man and his pigeon under his cap.

As the camera began to roll, he beamed as he explained what this unique, mutual bond with his pet pigeon meant. The story was aired on the evening news. Their strong, mutual bond of love was inspirational news for people to muse. The proximity of the bird under his cap gave his pet a sense of security. He was content being close to his pet parent in obscurity. Trust was complete, as being close to his significant other was a treat. Another pigeon would have immediately begun flapping his wings frantically in an effort to retreat.

When his pet pigeon dies, he will never feel the same during a race. It will take time for his life to resume its normal pace. The pigeon was close to his head under his cap. Between him and his pet's heart, there was no gap. When his precious bird dies, it will feel like his heart has experienced a brutal rap.

What his pet meant to him he will never forget. His memories at first may surface a painful blight. When he gradually heals, he will begin to recall memories that bring delight. It is natural that he will face the loss of his pet with dread. He will need to gradually face the reality when his pet is dead.

There is a special place for animal-human bonding that touches the heart and heals the soul. That is why so many people who have experienced a bond with a pet have a relationship that is more precious than gold. When a pet is lost, the grief journey often necessitates being heroically bold.

There are zoos across America because of humankind's love of animals. Now the surroundings in zoos are more like their natural environment with humankind's approvals.

It has been found that just looking at an animal is healthy, which is easy for us to see. When my granddaughter, Danielle, was three, she saw a giraffe that seemed as tall as a tree. Her eyes were enthralled with this amazing sight. She was astonished at the giraffe's color and height. As she was captivated by the animal, her pointed finger quickly began to rise. She wanted to make certain that her whole family saw this magnificent creature as she gazed at its beautiful brown eyes.

Animal rights are zooming as respect for animal-human bonding is accelerating. Humankind's attitude toward animals is increasingly venerating. Laws are increasing to protect pets, as the occurrence of abuse is alarming. Harming a pet is a felony. It would be criminally cruel to take away someone's significant life's melody.

How can anyone say that animal-human bonding is not a significant part of humankind's makeup? History has revealed how the bond has become increasingly complementary. Animals-human bonding has become humankind's increasing life's beneficiary.

To be touched is one of the greatest human hungers. Not to be adequately touched is a societal negligent, ominous blunder. It can be more dangerous than lightning and thunder. To survive and thrive, we need to be meaningfully touched or our lives can go asunder. Physical touch is the foundation for all of the other ways our lives can absorb life's wonder.

When I was born prematurely, I was put in an incubator for a month. The significance of touch was not recognized. Being touched was a rare experience for me. Cries yielded little response, and it felt like there was no one who cared an ounce. It took a long time for me to be comfortable with touch. Hugs are holistic, as they significantly aid in our physical, mental, emotional, and spiritual well-being. When we feel weak, affection can result in a physical, mental, and emotional resurrection.

A sense of playfulness plus affection together can enable our lives to blossom. A sense of frolic and a warm connection can give our lives musical rhythm. Together they can create a life that is enormously wholesome. Gaining an appropriate like cadence can help emanate a unique radiance.

We cannot stay healthy if we do not have a sense of play. Dogs and other animals invite our inner child to come out and have its say. We then can have fun until our lives experience the setting sun. I saw a bumper sticker that stated that it is never too late to enjoy your childhood. This statement is vital to be fully understood.

Playing is not an immature act, as it brings peace and relaxation to a very deep part of our soul. A dog lives for fun even when it is old. When my daughter was a young child, she said that every day was a good day for her and her brother. To me, these were words of gold that could not be adequately replaced by any other. To a pet every day is precious and playful and a sense of wonder.

It is not funny when humans do not allow fun and frolic to unfold. Children can give us permission to be silly which is like gold. My two-year-old grandson said, "Granddad, you are silly." He said these words affectionately and enthusiastically. This kind of silliness is priceless and can be relationally efficacious.

Without a respite of fun, difficulties can seem more drastic. Without a sense of play, we can more easily become frantic instead of ecstatic. We can miss a part of life that can be fantastic. An absence of fun can make life feel more caustic. On the other hand, with fun, our whole lives can become less static and more dynamic. More of life will seem to click, and we will not feel emotionally anemic. This genuinely and vitally lighter part of life is no gimmick.

You can increasingly feel the animal-human bond, which can give life an enjoyable kick. Laughter is the best medicine and can help heal a life's nick. Times of laughter can greatly reduce the full brunt of the pain when you have been emotionally kicked. You will not feel like the challenges of life have you licked.

The Animal-Human Bond Can Enhance Your Outlook

The animal-human bond can help you to look out for your outlook. You will be less likely to venture out into life and be shaken. An extraordinary outlook needs a journey within. Looking inward is a foundation for looking outward to begin. Looking out for your outlook necessitates that you take a second look. Animal-human bonding can be just what this deeper look took.

What is there to improved, add, or delete? Your pet's traits can help answer these questions, and your life will feel more complete. The deficits in your personality will not go untreated. When you bond with your pet, you will not feel cheated. You will feel that some frustrations in your life have been defeated. The bonding can produce future potential that has been seeded.

Journeying inward can help you venture out with purposeful actions, which will provide others additions instead of subtractions. Life can be about others as you have taken care of your needs. You will have the energy to support others when their hearts bleed. You will be able to reach out to the community and beyond and make the world a better place for goodness to spawn. The next day will become brighter as the sun begins to dawn. Taking a stand for another's excellence can be mutually beneficial and can last for a whole life long.

Your eyes will be looking out for a mission to accomplish. Your decisions and actions can provide an inner inspiration for others to flourish. Your empowered life will cause obstacles to vanish. Then you can move to help others who are experiencing anguish. Their minds, hearts, and spirits will no longer be famished. Their looking within will transform their outlook, and their lives will not languish. They will become inspired and live a life that they cherish. The flavor of their lives will increase as this inspiration adds garnish.

Look out for your outlook. Your ventures and responses will not make you appear like a schnook. An extraordinary outlook needs a journey within. Looking inward is the foundation for looking outward to begin. Human-pet bonding can help your outlook to ascend.

A Vital Aspect of a Healthy Outlook Is Hope

Pet bonding brings to many people's lives enhanced hope and purpose. A commitment to the well-being of your pet can help grant a meaningful surplus. Your pet can bring you hopeful inspiration by adding to the quality of your life. It can seem that the tough times bring less perspiration and less strife. The thirst for the meaning in life will be significantly quenched. Purpose and hope will not be benched. Your commitment to taking care of your pet can create a purposeful bond that is continually enriched.

The Seeds of Hope Can Be Planted within You from Unexpected Places

A joke that is circulating around is about a man who went to his doctor exclaiming, "No matter where I touch my body it hurts. Ouch! Ouch! See? Is there any hope, doc?" "Yes, surprisingly to you, hope will come from my ability to fix your broken finger!" For him, hope came from an unexpected place--the doctor fixing his broken finger.

No doubt, many of you have a memory of hope springing from an unforeseen source. As your horizons expand, hope can sprout and be strengthened in your life's course. In a sporting event, hope arose from a remarkably rare origin. When I was on a high school golf team on the final hole, I was faced with fast, downhill, curving 35-foot putt. The opposing coach remarked, "They will beat us 20-19 if Dan sinks this putt." My first reaction was for him to even think I could sink the enormously difficult putt made him seem like a nut.

Pondering this statement sparked hope and motivation for two different reasons: First, the coach's concerns inspired hope that the putt was sinkable. Second, motivation zoomed as I overheard that sinking the put would lead out team to victory which was previously unthinkable. The long, slippery, breaking put was solidly struck. The ball curved 15 feet to the right and fell into the center of the cup. We won 20-19, which was more than a stroke of luck.

In the game of life, you can expand your ability to discover hope from others, enabling you to cope. This increased vision can result in more focused determination to reach your goals' home bases. The cards in your deck of life can be filled with more aces. Regarding grief, hope from others can strengthen your endurance as you journey through the painful valley. Grief will gradually not feel like some dangerous dark alley, as you begin your energized life's rally.

Hope Can Come from a Passion Deep Within.

Second, regarding pursuing a goal, there may be virtually no outside support to enhance your vision's aim. The Wright brothers provoked laughter when they were striving to build a plane. People thought they were foolish. You may have experienced naysayers regarding your pursuing and achieving a goal. You may have begun to think that your goal was out of your control. You may have had to dig deep within to find treasures of hope. Increasing excavations deeply within can spark hope to begin and eventually you can win. You can journey to the end and experience good grief within.

Hope Can Surface from Inspiration from Others.

Gaining seeds of hope involve being inspired by others who have coped with the loss of a pet. You can become empowered by a hopeful mindset. You perhaps could reminisce at length about people who empowered you to persist. You were able to go the distance as hope overpowered any temptation to resist.

My identical twin brother's newspaper articles gave me a seed of hope that I could write creatively. This hope blossomed as I wrote 100 news articles that flowed naturally. This is my second published book. A nationally known counselor was impressed with my first book. Consequently, she gave me more information which inspired me to give life coaching a serious look. A few months later I quit my job to venture into this new expedition. I wanted to find out my unique creative life's rendition. This journey has been a creative exercise which has enabled my mind, body and spirit to increase it condition. The excitement of the journey is too great for words to begin to mention.

On one occasion while playing golf, I hit a shot in the woods. I had obstacles to overcome with seemingly no way out. I gained hope as I remembered attending a professional golf tournament. I watched as Arnold Palmer hit a golf ball into the forest. The ball seemed to be in jail with no opening to escape.

I was just 20 feet from Arnold Palmer as I saw his hawk-like eyes scanned around and above. He found a way of recovery and he knew that he could make this ball fly more skillfully than a dove. He quickly hit a shot with the correct trajectory and enough thrust to surge through some thin twigs in a huge tree. It flew up in the sky to its freedom and landed in the middle of the fairway as his plan set the ball free.

He saw the thin twigs, and they gave him hope. He could sense that the force behind launching the golf ball would be enough to bend the flexible twigs and allow the ball to fly through to its freedom. As my errant golf shot was imprisoned by trees, I remembered Arnold Palmer's remarkable shot flying through the trees and into the breeze. Inspired, I looked around and above to see if a way of escape could be seen. I soon saw two limbs parallel to each other with a small space in between. I gazed through the opening and could see the green.

I hit a 75-yard wedge shot between the limbs, and it flew to its freedom. Making full use of its miraculous escape, the ball bounced onto the lower tier of the green and rolled to the top level into the cup. Hope from Arnold Palmer's shot gave me more than a stroke of luck.

I recovered from the aftermath of the poor shot that landed in the woods. You can recover from the aftermath of grief and life's challenges with a hopeful attitude working for the good. Serenity gave me presence of mind while wisdom kept me from being blind. Courage gave me the will to follow through with the plan in my mind. I saw the light and overcame the blight with a possibility in sight. This possibility became reality as I followed through with a miraculous shot with delight.

Your bonding with your pet can become a priceless influence in your life. The smile of your pet can help you cope better with life's strife. Your pet can find fun in little things. This kind of fun can enrich your life like only a pet bond brings. This precious bond can fertilize your hope and energize your life like powerful recoiling springs. Because of this invaluable relationship, pet loss grief can begin a challenging painful grief trip.

You may feel imprisoned by the strength of grief's grip. As you begin to heal, enriching memories of your pet can strengthen your will. You can gain hope and freedom from the dark woods of grief as it begins to yield. The limbs can become twigs which enable you to cope. As you gain momentum, the twigs will yield and you will be free from grief's grip that felt like it was strangling your throat.

I am still inspired by the remarkable, sparkling smiles of a friend's dog. When he looked at me, his brown eyes penetrated my soul. As I think about this bond, I become more alert. Becoming more alert can help you not to be hurt. Your attention will not divert. The aspects of your life will be more like a harmonious orchestral concert. As a result, you will feel more stalwart.

Your focus will find a way out as you will have a wise inner scout.

The bond with your pet can provide priceless, innumerable benefits. With pet loss these benefits can be painfully missed. Your life had been relationally immense when your pet bond did exist. When death occurred, grief became a formidable challenge from the pain of what you missed. As the life of your pet enhanced your outlook, the death of your pet can seem like a cruel crook. The death of your pet can result in your feeing overwhelmingly shook. You now may not see the sparkles in a brook. Eventually with hope strengthening your outlook, you will know what you need to do to grow creatively through grief dark secluded nook.

Patience Can Powerfully Fertilize Your Outlook

Patience can bring prudence as you live alertly in the present. Patience can help you bathe yourself in life's essence. Your life will have a unique cadence, and you will feel that challenges and obstacles are less of a hindrance. You can have time to go inward as well as outward for guidance.

As a result, your life will have more substance. You will be less apt to experience wanting vengeance. Patience can breed wisdom by preventing unwise impulsive actions to prevail. Patience can give you freedom to grow and keep your life from feeling like it is in jail. Patience is not avoidance. Patience can allow you to stare life in the face and prevent a negligent consequence.

Patient thoughtfulness can help your life make more sense. As a result, patience can serve you well, and your mind will not be dense. Surpassing the speed limit of your grief's natural pace can leave egg on your face. You may feel a false sense of disgrace. It takes patience to walk through the valley. With patience, you can experience grief's recovery with dignity and your life can rally.

Patience can bring balance. The ability to be patient can surface in silence. Creative coping can bring healing within your grasp. Coping with grief by having patience can aid in this arduous task. Patience can aid in enjoying the journey and reaching your goal at last. Patience can bring clarity and guidance. You can be kind to yourself and allow soothing experiences to give you a healing, attitudinal stance.

Patience can foster persistence. In grief, you can keep on going through the valley without undue resistance. What you resist can persist. You can persist and not resist. Consequently, your grief can subside and barely exist. Patience can bring healthy periods of calm silence. You can grieve by yourself and not depend on others as your sole reliance. You will move through anger and not feel continual defiance.

Patience can be healings essence. You can live with the pain and not get caught up in the consequences of avoidance. Patience can bring continued allegiance. Then you can support your pain with compassion and dependence. Patience can bring steadiness resulting in your feeling a stronger sense of readiness.

Pet Bonding Can Enhance a More Purposeful Outlook

With pet bonding, you can have a significant purpose in life. This purpose involves giving your pet kindness and love. Your pet can provide purpose to your actions by resulting in a bonding that can brace you from life's inevitable shove. You can see the world through different eyes. Your pet enhances your aliveness as warm playfulness abides.

Conversely, with the loss of your pet, your outlook can be jolted. It may seem that much meaning in your life has been bolted. Your future purpose can feel blinded. By your painful feelings, you may feel hounded. Your emotions may feel ragged as you may feel that a vital blessing has been looted. Your sense of purpose can wane as you may feel that it has become brutally booted.

Your frazzled and frayed emotions can feel slighted. You may feel like you have a broken heart that cannot be mended. You may feel that much of your purpose in life has been lost. Going through painful grief, you may be chided. You may feel that it is hard for the lighthouse to be sighted, as your mind and sight may feel clouded.

All the assets of the bond with your pet fostered and can now feel like liabilities. Initially you may feel your fragility, and you may long for tranquility. You may wonder if adjusting to your loss has feasibility, and you may doubt your capability.

Consequently you may be focused on negativity, and you may be in a state of shock as you feel immobility. Coping with the challenge of grief is a great responsibility. When your pet was alive, you experienced the bonds assets. Now the loss can bring painful feelings of deficits. The initial painful feelings can feel like bullets. What others understand about your grief may feel like snippets, and your positive emotions can experience plummets.

Death brings many hurtful feelings that can be experienced as culprits. You may long for the day that you will begin to experience emotional summits. It will be nice when memories of your pet seem like pleasant visits. With valor in dealing with your grief, you can experience coping merits. You have the challenge of strengthening your adaptability. When you endure the journey and cope in the future, you can see your possibilities and potentiality.

Because pet bonding is so rewarding, pet grief can become alarming. That challenge of pet grief can be startling. It can be a long journey before your eyes are sparkling. You may be frustrated with the loss of deeply felt needs that you feel like barking. You can only begin to understand how intense pet loss can be by having some understanding of how beneficial the bonding can become.

With the loss of a pet, you may feel like a cat up a tree. How to plant your feet back on solid ground can seem like a mystery. You would like to find the master key to free you from grief swiftly. This next chapter reveals the extinct of the challenge of grief as your pet is now history. It reveals that the strong bond does not allow the grief journey to subside quickly.

You may not walk through the journey briskly. You may walk with grief's throbbing injury. Your steps will be more gingerly as the journey can feel slippery. With courage, wisdom, and endurance, you will begin to experience healings serenity. Then the loss will turn into victory. The memories will surface with meaning as the spirit of your pet will live on for eternity.

CHAPTER 2

The Challenge of the Grief Journey

Grief must not be held captive.
Grief must have the freedom to be active.
When grief is trifled,
Healing from your loss can be stifled.

Grief needs the attention it deserves
Then you can cope with grief journey's sharp curves.
Grief will not become the boss.
You can become the manager of your feelings of loss.

—*Dan Crenshaw*

B ECAUSE OF THE significance of pet bonding, pet loss has a powerfully painful impact. After the shock, you feel the loss and pain as an undeniable fact. Unfortunately, society does much to squelch the expression of grief. When one drives without a functioning muffler, one will eventually receive a ticket and suffer. When one does not muffle grief, society may give verbal warnings, which can hamper mourning's healing buffer. The resulting pain can become much rougher.

When I was ten years old, I saw a movie that depicted the Spartan army. In one scene, a huge man was dressed in a striking, colorful armor. His helmet, armor, and sword looked formidable and striking. At his side; was his eight-year-old son, who was all dressed up in military garb to his dad's liking. In one sense, the warrior's son was cute. His dad was trying to teach him to be a man and keep his vulnerability mute. His father took out his sword and sliced a huge gash on his son's right arm and did not give his son's suffering a hoot. He then looked at his son and said, "Now, that didn't hurt, did it?" The son silently grimaced and said, "No Daddy, it did not hurt," to avoid being given the boot. He was not entitled to express his pain, as he would be humiliated by his dad again and again.

The following poem and article expresses the strong pet bond and how others perception of the loss can be deceptively wrong.

A Thread of Gold--A Bond Untold

A thread of gold has no shape or form.
It is far from being a fabric that will adorn.
When a needle penetrates the golden thread
The fabric begins to take shape as it is artfully fed.

A pet bond begins with a seed to sow.
It needs to be cultivated for it to grow.
The fabric of Fido's friendship begins its journey to fruition
When they have mutually
Communicated with fertile conviction.

Then the pet friendship begins to thread its way
So the shape will mutually fit.
The bond is secure as the fabric of friendship
Is a thread of gold that has been skillfully sown.
The seed of the rich bond has been cultivated
As both pet and master have richly grown.

This thread of gold can be a bond that is untold
When loss occurs to others as fool's gold.

—*Dan Crenshaw*

Disenfranchised Grief Devalues the Impact of Loss and Increases its Challenge.

In recent years, the term *disenfranchised grief* has been used to refer to a grief that has no permission to express itself. As a result, grief can be chained to the heart and locked. One may not find the key. The individual's loss is not publicly recognized by others, sometimes not even by themselves.

Because the grief cannot be shared, these grievers face special pain and problems from which they should be spared. The demeaning attitude of society can result in their being scared. Their vulnerability is not wise to be declared. It can feel like by society they are impaired. Grief has them feeling snared. Unless they can find a caring person, their grief will remain undeclared.

With the emotional pain of grief gushing, society in general says the loss of your pet did not hurt, did it? Like the son who was cute, your grief can remain mute. One may ask, "When are you going to get over it?" Grief is a slow process of healing bit by bit. When you do not receive compassion, you can feel like you have been cruelly hit. You may never completely heal from a deep loss, and that takes true grit. Your life can still be strong and emotionally fit.

You can gradually return to the land of the living, aided by others who understand and are giving. A tragedy definitely tries the soul. The pain can result in you feeling old. You can cope creatively with the ordeal. Then with creative growth, the experience may not seem like such a raw deal. The trial can broaden your horizon regarding the human plight. You may eventually find ways to help others cope with grief's blight and experience a future that is bright.

You need to own and validate your grief and voice the pain of your loss. We have certain inalienable rights in America. One is that we have freedom of speech. We have the right to give grief full expression to not allow loss to become a leech. It is a part of the human experience, and creatively coping is not beyond reach. It is vital that a journey of healing become what you beseech.

The more that your grief feels like tsunami waves in the ocean, the greater you will need compassionate self-devotion. This will help calm your inner commotion. You will protect yourself from emotional corrosion and mental erosion. Your life will gradually experience locomotion.

A child may lose a pet turtle. The child has the right to be sad and grieve with support that is fertile. But striving to experience understanding may be futile. As a result, the child may learn that the way to deal with feeling grief is to stifle. The tortoise wins the race in grief, not the hare. It is a slow process, and a fast race may result in healings despair.

A family who has a child that was born with developmental disabilities often experiences chronic disenfranchised grief. Many years ago, I knew a pastor who said he needed two things when his child was born to gain some relief. He needed to celebrate the child that had been born. Also, he needed to express that not having a normal child brought feelings of being forlorn.

There are different developmental stages when grief surfaces again and again. A leader in the field of developmental disabilities was brought to tears from the chronic grief's demand. When his child was twenty-one, the feelings of grief that he would never have the option of having a family was difficult to stand. Thoughts that his son would never give him grandchildren came up again and again. Having a child with developmental disabilities may bring grief that will not mend. Along with the delights of the child comes the loss that is not mild, and the grief will not completely end.

Grief is real. It must not become disenfranchised and discounted. It can then become pain that is confounded. These feelings can be hidden as others see them as being unfounded. When a pet is lost, a person needs other people to know how much the pet counted. This loss can result in a person's feeling painfully dumfounded.

Healing can be enhanced greatly by sharing losses with people who are empathetic. When you are grieving, you do not need to be around people who are apathetic. Their token words may be synthetic. Genuine support can be healing and powerfully authentic. While there are great challenges there are some actions that can help the grief work to work. If you are a person who has experienced a devalued loss, it must be accepted that wherever there has been attachment, grief will occur. You can have their own private way of grieving.

You may go to the cemetery, which can induce painful mourning, resulting in healing. Journaling often helps soothe grief's painful feeling. During certain times of the year, the pain of loss may surface, which may be unyielding. You need to structure the day, but you also need to utilize the opportunity to give time for healing and grieving.

When you lose a pet, you need another person who will validate your grieving. You need to know that someone understands that your level of grief is true and that you are not deceiving. You do not need for the cost of pet loss to be discounted. Many people do not understand how grief can be so traumatic. Some may feel that the healing of grief should be quick and automatic. It may result in a grieving person's mind, body, and spirit becoming frenetic.

A calming presence is what you need. This attention can become a present that can help you to grieve. Then the grief will not be disenfranchised. A supportive person will embrace your grief with dignity and not feel that your pain is overpriced. No matter what the source of grief may be, a person needs to face reality. Any grief has the right to have its say. This freedom will help your grief journey to heal each step of the way.

Some unique circumstances give grief a muzzle. Why the community cannot give permission to grieve can be a puzzle. They do not understand that the grief is real, and the public will not respond to the griever's appeal. We need to own our grief and validate it in order for our grief to stand up and voice its loss. We have certain inalienable rights in America. One is that we have the right to grieve. It can gradually give a healthy reprieve. Regarding the importance of grief, one must not deceive. It is a part of the human experience that we inevitably receive.

A pet may have died during a disaster like a tornado, hurricane, or flood. A person may insensitively say, "Your family lived," but the pet bond felt like family blood. The family may grieve the loss of their pet in isolation. It may become a complicated grief, as normal support may not be available for consolation.

Disenfranchised Grief Can Include a Miscarriage and Increase Grief's Challenge

People may have lost a pet, along with many other losses that are devaluated. Regarding having a miscarriage, a person may comment, "It's not as if you knew the child." Yet this statement ignores that the grief was not mild. The attachment that was formed during pregnancy was a deep, heartfelt smile. These feelings can be intensified by their previous excitement, anticipation, and waiting. A support group can help in their anguishing feelings abating.

I once did a funeral for a couple who had lost quadruplets at birth. Some people may feel that the couple should have no grief because the quadruplets did not live on earth. To the parents, each one was more precious than gold, frankincense, or mirth. They could not put into words what each child was worth. They had a picture of each baby displayed. I worked to honor the level of their grief as I prayed.

When grievers are disenfranchised regarding their pain, many people may not be believers. When grief is disenfranchised, people may feel that others see them as whiners. Disenfranchised grievers often feel that other people do not feel that their grief matters. If you slip into shame and the grief is discounted, you can like grief is a vice.

The grief is shamed, and it can feel like no help will suffice. Difficult people can make you feel like you should put your grief on ice. The grief cost more when you are manipulated by bad advice. You wish that there were some answers that are precise. It is human to wish that there were some magical device.

You may feel like grief is overpriced. The grief costs more when you accept bad advice. To escape from grief is likely to entice. You wish there were some answer that is precise. People who do not take other people's grief seriously may need pointers. When grievers are disenfranchised, they feel that they are experiencing increased rigors.

People who discount others' grief may think grievers are fibbers. Disenfranchised grievers need supporters to serve as buffers. Disenfranchised grief may be demeaned as one suffers. People whose grief is disenfranchised may be seen as goners, gripers, and may experience their disposition as an imposition.

Triggers that Resurface Mourning Increase Grief's Challenge

Regarding a pet, it may be difficult to see someone playing with a dog, particularly the kind of dog that you had. You may miss that playfulness very much, and the pain can be bad. Missing that sheer delight of frolic can result in your being mad. People may mean well, but it doesn't feel like it helps even a tad. You feel very vulnerable, and your emotions may feel scantily clad. You cannot wait until you can again feel glad. Grief is real. It needs to be given a voice. You feel that you cannot even allow your eyes to become moist.

Emotions have a huge challenge in finding their way out into the sunshine. It may feel like your emotions do not know the way and are blind. The grief over the loss of a pet needs to come out of darkness into the light. Otherwise, it can become an increasing blight.

One thing that helps greatly in grief is sharing the losses with people who are empathetic. Not being able to discuss losses complicates grief and can result in life feeling pathetic. At best, grief is very difficult. When it is not given its due, it can have a dark hue. There are great challenges, but there are some things that can help the grief work to work. You may have experienced triggers, which increase rigors.

With unsupportive people, the grief needs strong boundaries to be hidden. People may not understand that the downward shift of emotions in grief can be sudden. Grief can be like a bucking horse that you have ridden. The downward plunge of emotions and expression may be forbidden and sudden. As a result, you may feel shame and guilt-ridden.

The challenge is great in finding allies that understand the ups and downs of the grief journey, which is normal in spiraling upward and out of the darkness into light. These allies can be on your side in the challenges of grief's fight. They will celebrate with you when the bucking horse becomes tame. Any remnants of grief will not result in your feeling lame.

The Challenge of Grief Can Be Helped by Grieving Alone.

To facilitate healing in your grief journey, you may go to the cemetery. In your grief journey, visiting the cemetery or memorial place may be necessary. Journaling often helps to keep grief from feeling so predatory. Certain times of the year can be difficult. The music of your life can become dissonant. It can feel like something else foreboding is imminent.

You may feel like you have to be overly vigilant. Life can become confusing and intricate. Your frustration can feel militant. You can find that your coping skills can be strengthened and you can become a hero's equivalent.

Dignity Regarding One's Level of Grief Can Aid in the Journey's Challenge

No matter what the source of grief may be, a person needs to face reality. One way to help is to give grief dignity. Finding a support group of people of like mind can be helpful as one is on a journey toward healing. One deserves dignity as grief grips one's soul and feels unyielding. Understanding gives one freedom to grieve and honesty about what one is feeling. In trying to be honest, people can say insensitive responses, and you may want to hit the ceiling. You can lean into grief by finding support from people that are appealing.

By giving yourself help, you can maneuver through the bumpy, jagged grief journey. You know that there is light beyond the darkness when your emotions feel stormy. Being in your supportive corner can prevent stress from shaming you as a grief-stricken mourner. You may feel like your heart is on the burner. People can lose patience with your grief and become sterner.

Regarding the grief journey, you may feel like a novice learner. Without dignity, the stress of grief can become magnified. The greater the anguish becomes, the more that your grief needs to be dignified. You may feel like part of you has died and your heart has been fried. Dignity can change from suffering to pain. In suffering, you feel like a helpless victim who is lame. With pain, you feel like you can become empowered to gradually feel heading's gain.

The Challenge of Grief Involves Managing Stress.

Too much stress can hamper life. It can put a damper on goals with strife. Stress can cut your heart like a knife. Calming thoughts can keep your life from becoming a mess. Serene thinking can renew your zest. Your focus will help you reach the crest.

Prevent Messing with Stressing

—Dan. Crenshaw

Prevent messing with stressing.
Your serene life can become a blessing.
Stress can dampen your life with strife.
Serenity can breathe within you the breath of life.

Prevent messing with stressing
Calming thoughts can help your mind to be at rest.
Serene thinking can renew your zest.
Your focus will help you be your best.

Contemplate a fresh stream.
Reflecting the rays of a sunbeam
Envision being splashed all over by a water fall,
Breathtakingly giving you a comforting shawl.

Envision a meadow full of flowers,
And how you would feel lying there for hours.
Envision a mountain that is majestic and strong
With a calm lake reflecting its beauty all day long.

Envision a rose garden in full bloom.
You will be relaxed very soon.
Every color of roses that you can imagine is there.
You are engulfed by roses that are everywhere.

The sweet smell of roses radiates a savoring scent
You are enraptured as your five senses are without a dent.
This experience has made your soul serene.
You have gained a glimpse of what true serenity can bring.
To be serene is to be like a ship coming into its harbor to dock.
To be serene is to be like character that is solid as a rock.
To be serene is like a sparkling new ship set free at sea.
To be serene is like a soul experiencing eternity.

You can allow your mind to go to your special place. Your mind, body, and spirit will experience a respite of grace. It is hard to be serene during grief, but finding ways to reduce stress can help grief work to function at its best. Developing and strengthening your ways in coping with stress will enable life beyond grief to be lived with excellence and zest.

Bereavement Has the Challenge of Moving from Darkness into Healing Light.

If the impact of pet loss remains in the dark, it can become toxic. This emotional infection can make you feel neurotic. With emotional germs running wild, you may feel chaotic. As time moves on, you may feel idiotic. The challenge is to receive emotional healing with human support as an antibiotic. The times of overwhelming pain can become less episodic.

An untreated, wounded heart can infect one's emotional and physical health. The abscess then is not lanced. It does not experience even a glance. No antibiotic is given, and the wound does not heal. The journey toward healing has been delayed at best, and grief will not yield.

Once, I went on a two-hour hike on a hiking trail at Superstition Mountain in Mesa, Arizona. As I was taking my last few steps toward the top of the trail, I slipped and nicked the back on my hand on a rock. It did not seem like anything significant, but quickly it became infected and swollen. I became sick.

In the middle of the night, the pain in my hand was increasing. I became very concerned. I went to a doctor and received a prescription for an antibiotic. As I took off the bandage in the latter stages of healing, I was alarmed to see a slender round splinter with a sharp end sticking vertically one inch out of the wound. It had penetrated the skin deeply and disappeared. It took a week for it to emerge and reveal that it was the infection's source.

The source of the infection was hidden, and as a result, complete healing was forbidden. Pet grief may seem like a small nick to others, but if unattended, you can become very sick. People may not see the seriousness of the wound to the heart. Grief needs to come to the surface and begin yielding the right way toward healing. The twig that was the source of the infection surfaced into the light. The infection then gradually became less of a blight. When bereavement can find a way from darkness into healing light, life can begin to feel all right.

Facing Reality and Letting Go Challenges the Task of Grief Work.

Facing reality feels surreal as the feelings that surface can seem like abnormality. As you experience healing from loss, adjustments can change your personality. Out of coping with the pain can come the promise of your potentiality. Getting to this point is not a formality.

Loss is facing life head-on and utilizing one's spirituality. Spiritual inspiration can energize grief's journey. Then one can begin to bring to life their full mentality. Discovering and enhancing the needed coping skills can enable you to deal with life's most difficult reality.

Consequently, grief is one of life's most challenging circumstances. While you may not heal from grief without leaving a trace, you can become more empowered to stare at life more fully in the face. Dealing with the pain and promise of grief can result in a life with more serenity and grace.

The next chapter deals with the dynamics of grief and the coping skills that can become grief healings match. Out of courage, coping skills can hatch. You can find some keys that will gradually open the door from grief's locked latch. By coping, you will not feel like the battle with grief is an overmatch. You can both heal and detach.

Grief may return again and again, feeling like a rematch. Then the grief battles have less fire and visit with less ire. It seems that finally, grief succumbs and begins to tire. In the tenth round, you can be pronounced as the victor. You will have stayed in the fight with creative rigor.

CHAPTER 3

Coping Creatively with the Dynamics of Grief

By having a basic understanding of grief's impact,
You can have a foundation to cope and keep your life intact.
Empowering your autonomy can enable you to cope with grief's dynamics.
As you cope with grief, your personality can become more dynamic.

—Dan Crenshaw

Being Autonomous is a Plus

BEING AUTONOMOUS IS a must. In God and in yourself you can trust. When disappointment comes, you must not allow your heart to rust. By using autonomous, creative, coping skills, you can adjust. As you encounter challenges, with yourself you can be fair and just. With a healthy sense of self, you can rebound and not feel disgust.

Autonomy can create sterling silver out of grief's emotional rust. When the strong, stormy winds come with a gust, spiritual and human support can give you a welcomed thrust. When you are ready to face reality, you will have gained the strength to face your loss in totality. Then you can have a creative foundation to tread the tearful waters of grief's brutality. You can begin your unique journey toward healing in actuality.

Autonomy is the foundation out of which adequate coping skills can emerge. By declaring your independence, your uniqueness can surge. You can have the freedom to reach out for help when your heart receives a huge dent. Someone can have a mission to come to your aid that is God-sent. When you have a healthy sense of self, it is more than a sentiment. Feelings, thoughts, and actions can fill the cracks in your foundational cement. It will help you deal with your real lament.

When you have a healthy sense of self, you can forgive others who have been unfairly fussed.

You will reach your goals with self-reliance that will not bust. You can gradually become comfortable in your own skin. You may lose a battle, but regarding the war, you will win. You mind, soul, and emotions will be on the mend.

You will have a compass that will give you direction in the storm. Your courageous actions will be far beyond the norm. You can create a life that is picturesque in form. Coping skills can help your heart become in tune. Your life's coping tuning fork can help you adapt to change. The melody of your life will enlarge its musical range.

The coping skills facing reality and letting go are at the core of grief work. Also, coming to terms with reality and letting go when it is appropriate are the essence of living the good life. Thus, grief work can become transforming as it can give more coping muscles.. Good grief work can lead one to greatness.

Coping with Grief Involves Letting Go and Saying Goodbye.

Memorial services can help mourners who have lost their pets to begin to say goodbye. Memories allow you to have the opportunity to begin to celebrate, honor, heal, and cry. By saying goodbye, you can gradually heal. The pain of grief will yield. You will no longer feel the sharp pains of grief's knife. Then you can say hello to the enriching contributions pet memories now bring to your life. You will have creatively come to terms with grief's pain. Now, loss has resulted in gain. As you begin to heal, memories can move from devastation to inspiration. The memories can become a soothing chime to your heart, soul, and mind.

The memorial service should be a natural reflection of the pet that one lost. Memories can be expressed. I attended the memorial service of one of my uncles. My uncle's best friend spoke of fond memories. He gave one character trait of my uncle that stands out in my mind. His friend reminisced and stated that he had been with my uncle through many life and business ventures. Through these experiences, a character trait that permeated my uncle's life was determination. He reported that he never saw my uncle dodge an obstacle. It evoked within me both prideful memories and healing tears. These memories have inspired me through the years.

My uncle's son picked up his traits. He was an architect in New York

City when the need for architects collapsed. His peers by the hundreds gave up their architectural careers. He went international by transforming his company into specializing in environmental architecture. As the architectural industry in New York took a crashing dive, his creative drive enabled his business to thrive. His son spoke with a sparkle in his eye about his memories and influence of his dad.

I played golf with my uncle virtually every Christmas. His caring presence brought out the best in my golf game. I became energized. I once hit a high nine iron from over 100 yards away from the hole that landed in the hole and made a dent at the bottom of the flag for an eagle--two under par for a single hole. I can still feel the love and warmth of his strong hands as he placed them on my head during my ordination service. He genuinely relished every breath of air that he inhaled. His legacy left footprints on my life.

He was an athlete and inspired me to lift weights in high school. This endeavor took my golf game to new heights. I shot a seventy-four, my lowest round in competition. I sank a 35-foot putt on the last hole and led our high school team to victory 20-19 as we defeated a high school much larger than ours. The memories that I have of my uncle at this moment boosts me forward. I write these words with some tears. At the same time, I relish the many memories that have inspired me through the years. How memories influence your life can be tangible and intangible. After you grow through the brunt of the pain, life will never be the same.

Many pets have enabled their pet parents to become more like the kind of people that they wanted to be. What traits of your pet have influenced your life? What traits do you remember and will miss? Many people's lives have been changed by the traits of their pet. You now may be able to give more unconditional love. You may have gained a greater sense of playfulness. You may be able to live life more in the present. You may be able to engage in more eye contact, as eye contact may have been natural for your pet.

Creative ways can be developed for you to express what your pet meant to you. The pet may have served in some specialized skilled service that helped enhance the quality of a person's life. The pet may have been a hunting companion with a myriad of meaningful outdoor experiences.

It may be the little things that you remember. I had a beautiful cocker spaniel that was white with light brown spots named Dutch. One of my fondest memories concerned his staying three feet behind my left foot as I jogged daily for four miles. After my pet's death, my jogging experiences were not the same.

Once a friend of mine wanted a dog, and I went to a pet store with her. She asked the customer service lady if they had a poodle. The person in customer service said that they did, but there was something wrong with the poodle's legs. He was very lethargic. She bought him anyway. The dog quickly demonstrated vitality. Without bonding, the dog was fast becoming a fatality.

I took care of this friend's dog for a week. I can still see this poodle becoming at one with the earth as he rolled down a grassy hill on his side. He was totally absorbed in this exhilarating experience. When my friend was preparing to move to California, I visited her dog for the last time. I was 200 feet from the pet of my friend, and he began to give me a welcome dance circling around in delight. I picked him up to give him a hug of goodbye. His whole body was thrilled at the closeness of my touch. I had to say goodbye to a pet friend. The memories I have of him gradually enabled my heart to mend.

A memorial service can become foundational for a person who is creatively moving through grief. A place in the yard of a house can be used for memories. Many personal and meaningful artifacts of the pet can be displayed. One can spend periodic times at the memorial place. These valuable moments of memory can surface grief. As one begins to heal the memories can help a person to relive the enriching experiences. These memories can then engender rich experiences in the present by allowing past memories to emerge from the fertile soil of the pet bond's past. Having a memorial service is not like waving a magic wand. The memories allow emotions to freely respond.

Also, it is important to recognize that clinging to all of the artifacts and memorabilia of your deceased pet can hinder letting go and saying goodbye. A few cherished items can be enough for you to grieve what you miss and later cherish what you remember. It is difficult to use the word *goodbye* in any situation. When a friend moves far away, every ounce of mental acuity may be used to avoid saying goodbye. One might say, "Our paths will cross someday." That may or may not happen. The reality is that one is saying goodbye to the relationship as it has been. The friendship will be missed.

When I was a chaplain intern, the director of the program said it was hard to say goodbye. After I finished my education and became a chaplain, he called me one day and said he was moving and wanted to tell me goodbye. I resisted by saying, "I will see you at the National College of Chaplain's Meetings." He knew that he was saying goodbye to the type of relationship that we had. He went on to say it again, "I called to tell you goodbye." The second goodbye registered deeply. It felt congruent to reality. It had a powerful impact as it helped bring closure to his leaving. Saying goodbye regarding pet loss can be vital in grieving. A few years later I did see him at a College of Chaplain's meeting. Having said goodbye to bring closure to the past relationship granted a solid hello to the present bond which did still exist.

You can write a letter to your deceased pet about the things that you miss or regret. Expressing these feelings is another way of letting go. Gratitude for what the pet meant to one's life can also be expressed in the letter. Gratitude for how your pet enriched your life is the other side of experiencing the pain of what you lost. There is then a need for a combination of remembering and grieving. The pet's name can be used at the beginning and end of the letter. The spirit of your memories of your pet will always be deeply imbedded into your heart. In that sense you will never be truly apart.

This letter can be written in segments if your emotions feel overwhelmed. First, you can acknowledge how your pet contributed to your life. The remembrances regarding how your pet added to your life can cause the grief of what is missed to surface. Seemingly small memories can be huge in the healing process.

As a result, you can gradually become energized. The stage is set for you to move forward toward greater excellence, purpose, and passion in every aspect of life. Creatively adjusting to your loss can present the opportunity of creating a total life design. You can renovate every room of your life resulting in a colorful, dynamic and energetic life.

Being able to let go is a good coping skill to begin to heal from grief and gain relief. Also, hanging on to life during the time of transition is paramount. The coping skills of letting go and hanging on are vital skills that can fertilize the quality of one's life; One's life can be filled with color and creativity. It can be consumed with purpose and passion. Learning to say goodbye is crucial in our life's journey. Letting go is the the cornerstone of dealing with grief's discord and moving towards harmony.

When my father was in WWII, he was drafted at the age of thirty. He was a small man, five feet six inches tall. He was a medic and had to carry heavy equipment. In an invasion where he had to scale a wall, he had to find a way to climb over it. He had to let go some of the baggage that was weighing him down. As a result, he was able hang on to make it over the wall. While realistically it is not generally possible to completely let go all of our emotional baggage, the skill of letting go helps us to get over the obstacles in life without insurmountable weight. The dual skills of letting go and hanging on are vital in coping with your grief and your life as a whole.

Saying goodbye can involve letting go of guilt, anger, denial, and gradually the pain of the loss. This letting go is often not an all-or-nothing experience. My father did not let go all of his equipment. He was able get over the wall by letting go part of his equipment. He could function as a medic with what he had left. As you say goodbye, it may not be an all-or-nothing experience. You may let go enough of the baggage to overcome the obstacles of future challenges.

I attended some circuses as a child. A trapeze artist has to let go one bar as he is swinging forward to catch the hands of the person on the other bar. We have to say goodbye and let go to be able to say hello to others and catch opportunities of growth as they come our way. The previous screeching sounds of grief in the mind can leave one aghast. Memories can eventually become enriching, musical echoes from the past. The musical memories can now invigorate your life, and your fulfillment can become personally unsurpassed.

Grief's Dynamics: From Denial to Creatively Coping with the Trial

The journey toward being able to heal enough to experience memories as musical echoes from the past can be a monumental task. At first, memories can create anguish that can leave one feeling incessantly harassed. Because of the explosive nature of strong, erupting feelings, denial is a merciful way of coping initially. Denial helps one manage the shock and prevents one's emotional system from becoming overwhelmed. Then you can move through the shock to eventually reach your ship's dock.

One often cannot deal with the initial full impact of the loss. Denial is not facing actuality. It is giving irrationality its needed time. Denial is not factual. It is temporarily merciful. It is a time that is needed to be irrational. It provides a shield from feeling the full brunt of what is actual.

How many emotional quakes can one deal with at one time? When does the excruciating, molten lava of the emotional pain call for a retreat?

You can step back when the pain is overwhelmingly deep. The initial, multifaceted aspects of grief can become like bullets penetrating your heart, mind, and soul. The ultimate effect could rip open the body without any anesthetic to cope with the gaping hole.

Denial and numbing shock can help prevent too much pain from engulfing people who are experiencing pet loss. Then one can heal at one's own pace. Grief is not like running in a race. It is gradually looking at reality squarely in the face. As a result, you can put your life into perspective with emotional intervals of space.

I have taken fitness training from a coach. The coach stated that when one's muscles begin burning, it is a sign that they need a rest. This escape is needed when the emotional, molten lava is burning at its crest. As a result, one can manage the impact of grief. You can gradually become less rattled and more settled. Then you will not feel so emotionally embattled. Many people during this time feel numb. This distance from the pain can help you not to succumb. A person who is usually gregarious may become emotionally frozen and mum.

People who have experienced trauma can slowly deal with the emotional aftermath and gain relief. You can gradually become less rattled and more settled when the pain is not so excruciating even though this journey may not be brief. Then you will not feel so emotionally embattled and can cope more effectively with your grief. Denial then is a temporary, merciful coping mechanism that enables you to brace yourself during the initial shock of the loss. As the fog of the shock begins to dissipate, you can begin to cope with the reality of your fate.

Experiencing overwhelming pain from pet loss is not an abnormality. To lean into reality, you can gradually experience grief's totality. It can take a long time before you experience your normal vitality. Many people attempt to assuage the pain of others by utilizing triviality. Discounting the cost of the loss can be a way for people to avoid facing the reality of their own mortality. You can gain comfort by having spiritual faith in eternity for you and your pet.

I used to be a chaplain for people with developmental disabilities. I was asked to visit a group home to help a resident to deal with his father's death. I asked one of his friends to go outside the door. Next, I asked him to come back in to help him with his grief more. I told the grief-stricken resident that his father went through the door and would not be coming back.

His six-group home friends came up to him and gave him hugs, which helped him to gain support. What a precious experience! His grief was given honor and dignity with no flack. He was able to grieve with support that often many people lack. His wounded heart came out of the darkness and was exposed to a healing, supportive light. Support can help empower you to gradually move through life with your full, energetic might.

When reality of a loss is faced, you may feel like sudden, stabbing sharp emotional pain may be experienced. When energy increases, you can be ready to gradually face the full impact of loss without interference. Healing slowly can begin to enable creative recovery's appearance. The ups can last longer and the downs can become briefer, resulting in grief becoming less intense.

It can be confusing to have ups and downs. The grief waves can eventually that you to shore.

Then the overwhelming pain of grief will not be immense.

Therefore, this recycling into deep sadness can be a normal part of the spiraling upward and out of the valley of grief. During my divorce many years ago, I went out to visit my brother in California and had a wonderful time. I came back home thinking I was over the hump of grief. Then I soon grieved more deeply than before. The energy of the enriching trip enabled me to have the energy to do deeper grief work and enhance the healing process. Now, the pain did not have to be denied. By dealing with grief, the pain began to gradually subside.

When denial fades away, reality comes to stay. Facing reality is healthy mentality. The pain of grief does not have to be denied, and the anguish can gradually subside. By gradually leaning into reality, you can gradually break through the denial of death's finality. The courageous journey can help you regain and enhance your vitality.

Letting Go Involves Dealing Creatively with Change and Transitions.

It takes a heroic grief journey for memories in the mind to gradually feel like a musical chime. Leaving in the meantime can feel like a mean time. Living in the meantime can feel like a lean time. As you are in the throes of grief, you are in a difficult transition and may not feel like a dime. Living in the meantime can make you feel lost. This time of transition can feel like a controlling boss. You may have lost control regarding circumstances that erupt. Living in the meantime does not have to be a mean time that can totally disrupt.

Living in the meantime can become an adventure as you can become free to explore new opportunities and places to venture. You do not have to forever feel intense loss. The mean time does not have to be the boss. As you adjust with new coping skills, you can explore paths for a new dream. While living in the meantime, endurance can reign supreme. Living in the meantime can feel like a damper. You may feel afraid and want to scamper. Brainstorming can take one's brain out of the storm. Brainstorming can create new ideas that go beyond the norm.

Living in the meantime can feel like a mean time as you like a part of yourself was lost resulting in great cost. When you gain a new perspective, transitions do not have to be mean. A new and different life can emerge, and you can gradually begin to beam. One does not have to feel stuck in the muck of a bad dream. You can become a good dreamer as you can take actions with emotional muscles that have become leaner.

Living in the meantime does not have to continually feel like a snafu. Living in the meantime does not have to result in one's being stuck and feeling blue. You can rise above the transitional situation and gain a more scenic view. Now, regarding the challenging transition, your attitude can renew. The transition does not have to become an impossible imposition. Creatively coping with change can put you in a better position. Living in the meantime can seem brutally mean. You deserve support, and then beyond grief, a renewed life can reign supreme.

I was in a serious car accident when I was thirteen. The recovery seemed brutal, with many of my injuries hurting much worse than a sting. One of my many injuries was a broken arm. I had a cast on my arm for two months, and I later felt a sense of alarm. The muscles in my left arm shriveled up like I was disarmed. I could not straighten it out when the cast was taken off. I exercised my grip on my left hand and used it to screw bottle caps off. It became much stronger than my right hand and helped my game of golf to expand. I was able to tee off and send the ball further aloft.

With loss and grief, one's emotions can be fiery. Internally they may feel briery. Allowing grief to take its course can enable your emotions to not be as hoarse. They will carry with them a mighty coping force.

Coping with Grief Dynamics Involves Dealing with Anger.

Although not everyone may experience anger, this unwanted emotion can be a natural expression of emotions in the grief journey. People often think it is wrong to ask why. They think that it is an affront to God. That is a person's choice, but asking the question that has no real answer is a part of the shock. Asking why can be part of the grief journey's angry cry.

While Christ was suffering on the cross, he asked God, "Why have you forsaken me?" (Matthew 27:46). He also was able to say, "Father, forgive them for they know not what they do (Luke 23:34). We often become angry when we are baffled with life's unanswered questions. Losing a pet was something that filled a deep need within you. It can be a natural response to become angry when the fulfillment of a vital need is lost. Anger can surface in various ways congruent with the uniqueness of each person's personality. To the human heart, it makes no sense that such a precious animal should die. Forgiveness is difficult but can become part of the process of healing, especially in some circumstances such as your pet being murdered.

When you suffer, others may try to give trite answers to serve as a buffer. These friends can indirectly make your grief rougher. Such simplistic responses can surface more anger. At this point, it is certainly not helpful to lecture, "You should have realized that your pet had a short life span." That can be the kind of information to give a person at the time they obtain a pet. This pain can help grief to become somewhat offset. Thus, the grief from pain can be painfully met.

It is vital for a person to gradually let go of the anger and allow grief to take its natural course. As a result, continually asking why will cease, and your emotional voice will not become hoarse. The why questions will gradually fade and die even though one may still have times that they cry.

Anger can be expressed in many ways. One may be angry at oneself, the vet, God, or another person. Some of the anger may have some justification. But much of the anger is a part of the process, and the feelings of anger need to be honored and expressed in a manner that helps a person along the painful journey of grief. "Why, Why, Why did my precious pet have to die?"

The quest for an answerless question can create a life emotionally filled with chronic, painful indigestion. The quest is difficult to digest. It is not natural to lay an unanswerable question to rest. The mind may relentlessly strive for an answer that will bring peace, but the question's answer will not release. If the questioning does not subside, the need for the answer will hinder healing from pet loss grief. The energy is wasted on trying to find answers to answerless questions rather than healing from the pain of the grief itself.

Answers to life's most perplexing difficulties, then, are often not there.

Dan Crenshaw

It is not good to continually be caught up in the dragon's questioning lair. Being scorched by the dragon's fire may increase anger's ire. Answerless questions can bring uncertainty, resulting in a suffocating scare. A question that has no answer can be like an inoperable cancer. Unreleased angry emotions can spread over the heart, mind, and soul. Living with anger can result in one feeling old.

The nightmare of unanswered questions can be dark, and moving around in this darkness may be reduced one to a grope. It becomes a challenge to find hope. One may feel that they are at the end of their rope. One may ask, "Where is the light that can give the way out? The road is a maze and where is the scout?" It becomes natural to want to shout. When no answer comes, that shouting can help diminish the pain to a mild yelp. By releasing anger, grief will be appreciative of your help. Therefore, it is normal for why questions to surface. Your mind can be baffled at the answer's silence. "Is there no one that can bring reliance?" Your mind may have the attitude of relentless defiance. As a result, your mind may need some healthy guidance.

The Attitude of Being on Top can Make the Why Questions Cease

The answer can come from a shift of your vision, like the five-year-old child who was under a 250-pound man. He found a way to a positive, attitudinal stance. He did not hide his mind in the sand. He did not continually ask, "Why are you on top of me?" He said, "I am on top of you in my mind." That attitude came just in time. This attitude of being on top helps the incessant energy draining and churning in the mind to gradually stop. The unanswerable question is still there. The coping attitude that you are on top in your mind can slay the dragon in his lair. You can become free from the dragon's snare. You can find people who care.

You can accept what you cannot change. Being on top in your mind can keep your emotions in a healthy range. You can discover a life that can live with unanswered questions. You can be relieved of having extreme emotional indigestion. You no longer need to listen to suggestion after suggestion. The answer may come, but it most likely will not. To gradually lay the questions to rest is a wise journey's plot. You can gradually change your vision from being a vulture's victim. The suffering that put you in a helpless state can turn into pain, where you can find an open healing gate.

Letting go unanswered questions can allow you to live in the now.

Regarding finding the answers, you no longer need to know how. You have accepted what you can change and accepted what you cannot. Your nerves have been freed from their paralyzing knot.

Grief Dynamics Can Involve Coping with Regrets: Anger Turned Inward

Regrets can be a form of anger turned inward. If these regrets linger, your life can go downward. There can be different degrees of regrets. Guilt can be a part of the grief process. The guilt may come when one is not guilty. One may feel false guilt and put oneself in prison for a long punishing sentence. Continued guilt can become grief journey's huge hindrance. You can lose the freedom to heal with guilt's paralyzing infringement.

You may torture yourself unfairly by saying, "I did not do enough." Then grief can become more intensively rough. When I was eleven years old, I had a parakeet as a pet. Often I would allow the beautiful green-winged and yellow-breasted parakeet to come out of its cage in the kitchen. It loved to peck on apples.

Our house was being renovated at that time. A worker opened the kitchen door for a brief moment. In an instant, the parakeet seized his opportunity and flew outside at the very top of a pecan tree. I felt there was no atonement. I began to feel like an irresponsible louse as I did not protect the parakeet as the workers were renovating the house. This beautiful bird experienced this moment as monumental. It relished its freedom and the view. Regarding the plight of its future, it had no clue.

As the colorful bird perched at the top of the tree, it chirped at the top of its lungs as it felt free. It had never experienced such freedom and delight. It had no idea that death was imminently in sight. Delight would soon turn into dismal fright. This beautiful, delightful parakeet had no skills to make it on its own. In my grief and shame, I began to moan.

I had to let go of the guilt and forgive myself. If I did not, my whole life would have been put on a shelf. I did not think the parakeet would take such a quick opportunity to fly. I could not even imagine that it would ever die, and I began to cry.

When guilt becomes infected and worsens, it can turn into shame. If guilt or false guilt is not released, it can brutally maim. Taming the shaming malaise is difficult to obtain. It is deep feelings of being worthless with no value to gain. Shame chews up one's self-esteem and spits it out.

Then one's esteem is in shock and cannot scream and shout. Sometimes one can get stuck in shame, which is guilt gone wild.

A person may be shame-based from being abused as a child. People who have a shame-based personality may have a particular challenge in gaining peace. This shame may make difficult feelings of false or real guilt to be released. Negative feelings can grow deeper into feeling helpless, hopeless, and worthless as the power of shame can amaze.

Shame then sets one's heart ablaze. To be shame-based can create developmental delays as shame can place one's mind in a daze. To experience shame can be more than a phase. Life can become a complex, confusing maze. Mistakes can continue to replay, and a person can stay in an emotional malaise. Shame can be an emotion that betrays.

False humiliation can result in an attitudinal, damaging mutilation. This aspect of shame can result in negative rumination that resists cessation. A continual feeling of shame can result in one's life's stagnation as they mercilessly continue their false self-accusation. Your may lose your compass and wisdom in your life's navigation. As a result, it may prolong you from reaching your destination of restoration.

You may feel that you have not made a mistake. You may feel that you are a mistake. Then you may come to the conclusion that there are no redeeming virtues to make. The lights are out in this crucial aspect of life's game. Living in the darkness of shame is taking the total weight of needless blame. Shame then can result in one feeling lame. Grief's teeth can bite and deeply maim.

The winds of grief can feel more blustery. Shame can make grief seem scarier. To feel false guilt can make you feel more queasy and shaky. Shame can make grief feel like an even greater calamity, and as a result, you can feel sulky. To feel humiliated is to experience self-enmity. You may feel demeaned and then have an attitude toward yourself that is mean. Who you really are is not what it may seem.

Guilt can be good in helping you to grow toward being a better person. We can learn from our poor choices and move away from evil. Our mistakes can become stepping stones. On the other hand, shame can put us on a downward slide. One may experience healing as one has cried. Shame is a distorting dynamic that always lies.

The feelings of shame can come from abuse and trauma. It can prick and perpetuate the pain of a past tragic drama. This sense of disgrace preoccupies one with exaggerating one's limitations. A sense of worthlessness can blind one to one's possibilities. Shame may say that you deserve to be stuck in the anguish of grief. This feeling of humiliation falsifies one's worth and gives one no relief. It negates the reality that we are priceless. Shame can infect the mind, body, and soul and become relentless.

Taming the Shaming Malaise

When the shame is tamed, it can be harnessed. With the controlling bit in shame's mouth, one will no long feel bitten with one's life going south. One can bring treasure out of what feels like trash. One's self-esteem can become free of shame and bring emotional cash. Pain will then have a different texture and will not bash.

One can gradually heal as shame stops lashing the wounds. Then coming to terms with grief will not take endless moons. The eclipse of the sun will be over. The shining light will set one free from darkness's dreadful cover. The bright light will put shame to shame and spark one to recover.

Years ago when I was a chaplain intern at Baptist Medical Center, I saw a painting displayed in the hallway beyond the foyer that grabbed my attention. It was a painting of a forest that had been blackened by the blaze of a ferocious fire. Soot and embers were everywhere. I pondered what the painting could mean. Then I saw at the bottom-right corner a small budding flower.

We can more positively reframe how we interpret the experience that this painting depicts. It is natural to focus on the blackened forest and allow it to dominate one's life, or one can see that it was blackened by ferocious abuse resulting beyond one's control. The victim got in harm's way and chronic, inner pain naturally resulted. Their dignity was scorched and insulted. The budding flower on grief recovery has resulted.

Serenity can become one of the amenities of acceptance of oneself. This peace in your soul is a priceless trait. Your soul can open its gate. One can become comfortable in one's own skin. Shame will no longer be there to wear one's dignity thin. One can move from feeling like hell to more like heaven within. Freedom from false humiliation, guilt, and shame can allow grief recovery to begin. Dignity and serenity will be replaced at shame's end.

Dignity can help you realize that your life matters. You can gain creative, coping skills to deal with life's matters. You will no longer feel in tatters. There is a company where one can order dead roses that can be sent as a gag gift to someone that one does not like. Shame sends a gag gift that can gag the mind, heart, and soul. Then the gagged soul may live in quiet desperation. Shame makes one emotionally and spiritually homeless. They do not feel at home with themselves while they are in shameful distress.

Shame deprives one of purpose and meaning. It leaves the soul silently screaming. Shame makes one attuned to the people who are jeering. When the shame is gone, one can then hear the people who are cheering. Shame puts a sign on one's backs that says, "Kick me." A sense of dignity can give one a kick out of living, resulting in glee.

Dignity can help the journey of grief to be a less bumpy ride. Dignity frees one from shame and the need to hide. Shame makes grief gloomier. Dignity enables grief to be handled more bravely, and your life will feel roomier. Shame allows others to infiltrate your boundary. Dignity can keep people from violating your emotional territory. You can gradually feel victory as the bulk of your anguish has become history. Shame exaggerates the anguish of your pain. Dignity helps you to lean into your grief with an accurate aim.

Dignity Can Become an Antibiotic for Toxic Perfectionism.

Perfectionism can become a symptom of shame. When one fails, there is a torrent of self-blame. You can feel deeply ashamed. Treating yourself in such a cruel manner can cause you to be mentally maimed. Then failure must be avoided at all cost. With one mistake, one can feel lost. One may always feel like they come up short, as one cannot get perfectionism to abort. Perfectionism inhibits one from changing what one can change. One may fear the change will not be in their ability's range. To give one's best effort is frightening at best. It may be terrifying, which may squelch one's best healing quest.

Perfectionism and shame go hand and hand. This devilish duo creates a disturbance among people all over this land. Serenity is infected by these rogues. The Serenity Prayer can drive out shameful feelings in droves. Perfectionism can be defeated by the Serenity Prayer. Accepting what cannot be changed will not be as hard to bear. Courage will fight the shame within and help one to risk and begin.

Perfectionism infects peaceful serenity. When a mistake is made, it can feel like a gash in one's heart. It makes it more difficult for one to learn from the mistake. It is important for one to take dead aim at one's goals, but it does not have to be all or nothing. No one can change a past mistake. A mistake can become a stepping stone. Perfectionism can hurt to the bone.

Perfectionism can be incessant. Many sports figures have made a mistake and winning became a lost cause. The coach may use the words, "Shake it off." The coach realizes that if one continues to think about the past mistake, they will not be able to get their mind on the next game when they come through the gate.

If one golfer misses one shot, he will not hit the next shot well if he is still punishing himself for the mistake. With perfectionism, one feels that they never reach the pinnacle. As a result, one can become very cynical.

You have the challenge to accept the things that you cannot change and not be emotionally lame. Then you can pick yourself up, shake off the dirt, and be ready for life's game. Then the thoughts of the mistake will not hold you hostage. You will be free from bondage. Your mistakes can fade into the background, and you can become emotionally sound. With grace and serenity, one will not be preoccupied by past failures. One will be occupied by the hope of future treasures.

Coping Through Learning to Be Perfectly Imperfect

Being perfectly imperfect allows mistakes to serve as stepping stones. When someone has to be perfect, you hear many moans. Perfectionism is a tyrant that paralyzes with fear. To have to be perfect will keep you from going after the dreams you hold so dear. To have to be perfect gives a mistake the power that can result in a heart quake. To have to be perfect can keep you awake. Being perfectly imperfect gives you the opportunity to learn. Being perfectly imperfect keeps you from having heartburn.

Being perfectly imperfect allows you to dive into the waters of life. To have to be perfect sets you up for an unending inner strife. Being perfectly imperfect helps you to get up when you fall.

When you have to be perfect, your moving forward will stall. When you have to be perfect, with every fault, seeking your goals will come to a halt. When you have to be perfect, you cannot see yourself as you are. You may rationalize, become defensive, and keep people afar. Being perfectly imperfect allows mistakes to serve as stepping stones. When someone has to be perfect you may hear many moans.

Being perfectly imperfect allows for you to have unconditional love.

Being perfectly imperfect provides the peace that is symbolized by a dove. Being perfectly imperfect allows you to have a learning curve. By having to be perfect, your life may not survive the swerve.

Being perfectly imperfect strengthens the will. To have to be perfect can make one ill.

To be perfectly imperfect helps one to forgive. Having to be perfect, one cannot really live.

Being perfectly imperfect, one can thrive. To have to be perfect, your life can take a dive.

To be perfectly imperfect allows one to be energetic. Having to be perfect can give you the feeling of being pathetic.

Being perfectly imperfect, you will not be filled with regret. Having to be perfect keeps you mistakenly stuck as you cannot forget. Being perfectly imperfect provides a life that excels. Having to be perfect can be like a prison where one dwells. Being perfectly imperfect allows mistakes to serve as stepping stones. When someone has to be perfect you may hear many moans. Perfectionism is a tyrant that paralyzes with fear. To have to be perfect will keep you from going after the dreams you hold so dear.

Being perfectly imperfect can provide you the freedom to live in the now. Having to be perfect prevents a person from knowing how. Being perfectly imperfect helps one's life to flow.

Being perfectly imperfect enables one to go on. The last stage of grief is coming to terms with grief. It has been called "the acceptance stage." I like to use the expression "coming to terms" better, since complete acceptance may not be reached.

One may never completely get over grief. Coming to terms with grief occurs in the grief journey when grief is no longer staring one in the face. It has faded into the background as it has barely left a trace. A memorial service is a good time to begin to say goodbye and gradually let go. Memorial services allow the reality of death to begin to sink in. The slow healing process is set free to begin. One can remember what contributions one's pet has made. Then foundation for grieving what one has missed has been laid.

Patience Grants Wisdom

Patience can bring prudence. To have patience can prevent grieving from feeling like a worthless nuisance. Patience can help one move toward healing, which can be a long distance. As a result, patience is not negligence.

Patience can bring a sense of balance as well as enhance one's presence. Patience is not quittance. To be patience can bring clarity and guidance. Patience can be like a relaxing fragrance. Patience can enable persistence. Patience can bring healthy silence. To be patience can foster reverence. Consequently, patience is not a hindrance.

Patience can avoid needless stridence. To be patience can result in decisions of substance. Patience can prevent one to be stuck in a grievance. Patience can promote the bulk of grief's riddance. Patience can be healings essence. To be patience can result in brilliance. Patience can foster endurance. To be patience is the essence of good sense.

Patience can bring continued allegiance. To be patience can ward off divisiveness. Patience can prevent making a mess. Patience can bring steadfastness resulting in steadiness. Patience can prevent negligence. Patience can avoid nonsense. With patience, we will not experience grief's resistance. With patience, one can develop higher wisdom and sense.

Purpose Strengthens Your Ability to Cope.

Discovering your purpose in life is needed as it may have been disturbed. Losing purpose with the loss of a pet can make you perturbed. Losses can become an exploration as to your purpose in life. It is a time of reevaluation of your life and making adjustments. You may have lost a great sense of purpose when you lost a precious pet.

To lose a sense of purpose can intensify the seemingly brutal and mean grief. Gaining a sense of deeper purpose can give the pain of grief relief. Not having a sense of purpose can be detrimental. A sense of purpose can be instrumental. A sense of purpose is fundamental. A sense of purpose can become monumental. A sense of purpose regarding life can be ornamental. A sense of purpose can free you from depleting energy by being judgmental.

Meaning Can Help Transitions Not to Feel So Mean.

It is mean not to give life meaning. Without meaning, your mind may begin screaming.

Bringing meaning evokes purpose within and gives out positive energy to inspire others to purposefully begin. Becoming a cynic can leave your emotions screeching. If a cynic has goals, they are meaningless and far-reaching. A cynic does not want to find meaning. It is mean to you and to the world to not find some purpose. What is happening may give no answer and could be mysterious. Instead of interpreting life with meaning, you may say, "Life is preposterous." At times, your purpose may not seem clear. Some difficult events may seem senseless especially when they are near.

Meaning can help one to live with the questions when there are no answers. If you have no purpose for your life, it is like your body is filled with cancer. Your behavior will seem like a treadmill going nowhere. You will not have strong willpower that can get you meaningfully there. You may have a chronic expression that scours. That expression can create a life that sours. It can wilt the beauty of every flower. It can hide the sunlight and bring out meaningless and never-ending fright.

People's search for meaning is personal and unique. This meaning and purposeful search can provide a positive lifestyle technique. Then the journey will give you meaning as you move toward the destiny you seek. It is mean not to make like meaningful. Your behavior, thoughts, and feelings mean that you are making life purposeful.

To live life with a purpose gives life direction and meaning. To have purpose is to have a vision and a mission. To live with yourself as you encounter challenges you can be just. With a healthy sense of self, you will rebound and not feel disgust. Purpose brings fulfillment to the mind, body, and soul. Living with a purpose has a specific intention. Living with a purpose brings priorities to one's attention.

Without a purpose, we are walking in the dark. We react to what is happening and become a ship without a rudder. When we realize what we have done, we may shudder. When we react instead of act, it may result in a destructive blunder. When we react instead of act, we may end up asunder. When we act intentionally, we can become an ambassador.

When we react instead of act regarding our actions, we may become puzzled and wonder. When we react instead of act regarding our goals, we may blunder. When we react instead of act in relationships, we may become an intruder. When we react instead of act, we may have to run for cover.

We need purpose to cut on the lights to see where we need to go. Then we will not be like a ship that is tossed to and fro. A lighthouse will guide the ship safely to shore. The ship will ship out cynicism and grant purpose galore. Purpose spawns creativity and options to increase more meaning. Purpose can occur when you console a friend whose heart is sore. What gives you purpose is what stirs your passion about living. What brings you purpose is what motivates excellence in living.

Motivation can increase when we see the purpose's ultimate impact. This empowerment will undergird hope and keep it in tact. Purpose can keep a person's behavior on track. Having a passionate purpose can lead to breakthroughs. Your thoughts, feelings, and actions can overcome obstacles that renew. Having a purpose can keep one from engaging in continuous and meaningless chatter. Living on purpose can bring many healthy behaviors in your life that matter.

To have a purpose helps you to find creative, workable solutions. Then you can be committed to your purpose's devotions. Your life will not be filled with meaningless motions. With purpose, you will use your head for ideas that are aloft. Then the direction that you have sought may not be far off. Someone with a strong purpose has focus in their eyes. Their life is authentic and not filled with lies. They live in the present moment with meaning that prevents frustrating sighs. Their clarity of purpose can bring a sparkle to their eyes.

It is mean not to give life meaning. Some people try to make meaning out of scheming. Deep purpose comes from a depth of exploring the world and yourself. Manipulation and connivance put meaning on a shelf. For one's life to have meaning, it is important to have a healthy sense of self. Often it takes exploration for meaning to come in time. Patience can be a virtue to allow meaning to brew in your mind.

A Vital Coping Skill Is Accepting What You Cannot Change

The last stage of grief has been called *acceptance*. Grief is accepting what you cannot change. Regarding calling the last stage of grief as *acceptance*, I have felt reticent. I call it coming *to terms with grief* because the healing of grief may never be quite complete. Grief is basically behind you, and you have experienced a high percentage of relief.

You first have the challenge of dealing with the full impact of grief at your own pace. Then the challenge remains to learn to live with the remnants of leftover grief that are left for you to face. You can manage any milder remnants of grief. As a result, you can gain quick relief. You can manage your life after your loss, as you have adjusted to what it has cost.

Special times and places may cause sadness to surface. Walks along the beach may bring up memories of your dog that ran with profound gladness. To remember your pet's exhilarating experience may not bring to you jubilee. Now, at the beach, you may feel like a cat up a tree. You seem out of place with your pet not there for you to see.

Because your grief work works, you will not continually feel these encroaching, temporary hurts. These milder grief feelings can reveal that your grief healing attitude works. Grief will not hold you hostage and hamper your future quest. You will be able to soon scamper manifesting your renewed zest. These remnants of grief feeling will be just a small damper in your healthy, emotional quest.

Coming to terms with grief occurs in the grief journey when grief is no longer staring you relentlessly in the face. Grief has virtually stopped, and you no longer feel its hounding chase. It has moved into the background as it has diminished to a barely visible fade. A new life is now ready to begin to be made. Being stared at by another person can be uncomfortable. Being stared at by grief can be formidable. This bullying stare that is a rude, demeaning glare will no longer wear out your heart. Then coming to terms with the loss and no longer feeling like your life is coming apart.

If grief has been your boss, it has lost its job. Grief has no power to rob. You are now the executive of your life. You are responsible for making your life bright. When you have come to terms with grief, letting go has become basically complete. There is now a sense of peace and relief and that feels near. Recovering from grief has been a heroic feat. The arduous, healing journey has brought you closure, and your pet grief is in your emotional backseat. A new chapter can begin to unfold and bring you a real treat.

The liberty of the free speech of grieving can help one to gradually pursue "life liberty and the pursuit of happiness." To have free speech of grief can bring you healing and peaceful rest. A supportive environment has helped you to successfully digest emotions. The bark of grief has virtually stopped, and you have climbed the mountain's crest. Out of the painful sadness can spawn the promise of a life revived. One has become a person that has done more than survive. One can find that their lives can actually creatively thrive.

You have grown creatively through grief into a new stronger person. Healing from the grief has prevented devastation, and your life did not worsen. You gradually stopped grief on it tracks. You are now ready for creative impactful acts. You are free to creatively move from grief to greatness and live life to the max. Your life has become more dynamic, and you can peacefully relax.

CHAPTER 4

Factors That Can Increase the Intensity of Pet Loss

Pet loss can vary greatly in its grief intensity.
Many factors from the past and present can affect grief immensely.

—Dan Crenshaw

G RIEF COMES IN the slice of one's life situation. The ingredients in your present life can give energy to the grief restoration or present a challenge for overcoming devastation. This unwelcomed guest may visit you for a long time. Enrichment can give you energy to cope. Previous or concurrent stressors can result in your fragile hope. As you begin your unique journey, look at yourself in the mirror with compassionate eyes.

The size of your challenge can increase if additional difficulties arise. The sum total of these extra stressors can affect the intensity of your unique grief level. The greater the intensity level, the harder you will have to wrestle. Dealing more effectively with the added stressors can help lessen grief's fight. Then you will not look at the monster of grief and take flight. You can conquer grief as you courageously fight.

Uncertainty Regarding Pet Loss Can Inflate Grief's Intensity

Life is general is uncertain. Uncertainty intensifies when a dog is lost behind life's curtain. Whether he may have been stolen, had run away, or have been picked up by someone is not certain. Your pet may have gone away to die in seclusion. There is a famous, long-used statement that says, "Hope for the best and prepare for the worst.

You hope that if your pet is hurt that he is being nursed. Hope can keep one going and can help quench meaning's thirst. Straining to hear the answer to your questions can make one's eardrums about to burst. Has your dog been unwillingly coerced? You will do all you can to find your pet. When all that can be done is finished, you will have no reason to regret.

Uncertainty has many painful facets. If only is a guilt reaction dealing with the uncertainty. You may say that if things would have been different, your pet may not have experienced a disappearance. You have the challenge to deal with unanswered questions with an emotional, stable stance. Your real feelings may be blunted.

By becoming your worst enemy, you may feel affronted. The answers may or may not come. In the meantime, it is a huge challenge to deal with emotions that may feel glum. Living with questions is a part of life's scope. Creating new coping skills can bring purpose and hope. Faith in life will still exist as the temptation to be cynical will not persist. Your life can heroically subsist. You can creatively unfold even though the answers to your questions may be put on an indefinite hold.

Grief can feel very brutal. Spoken words that do not fit can feel futile. These words can become noxious to the soul and allow grief to enable one emotionally and physically to grow old. One can continually feel emotionally dead. Facing each day can become a dread. With a recovering attitude, one can gradually become alive instead. It can gradually enable one to recoil out of bed. One faces the day with hope and possibilities that are ahead.

The process of grief at its best can be gruesome. The challenge is keeping on the painful journey with courage that is awesome. Some people may try to steal your grief. Without the journey through grief, there can be no relief. A person who strives to take your grief away will hinder your purposeful relief.

People may want to minimize your grief as an insignificant fender bender. You need someone to understand and help you and become a caring grief mender. Many people may attempt to assuage the pain of loss by utilizing triviality. In not facing the reality of pet loss, one may try to avoid facing one's own mortality.

Making the decision to put a pet down can enlarge the grief dynamics.

It can be a difficult time to decide when your pet's life is ready for its ending time. It seems that most pets enjoy life even in the midst of much sickness, but there comes a time when they are ready to let go. Then comes the challenge of the pet owner letting go. This is a tough decision that can intensify grief. Information gathering from the Vet and your intuitive feelings for your pet can help in the process.

Lynda Trunnell gave me permission to share these creative thoughts which seems to accurately penetrating the mind of a pet during their last days:

I'm a little dog with curly hair. I have one eye, but I don't care! My knees don't work very well. I have to be carried everywhere. I get two shots every day. It's not fun, but it's okay. I feel good enough to play! It's not good that I can't run, but that doesn't hurt all my fun. I shake my toys very hard. They fly through the air way to far! Squeaky toys are what I love. I love treats too and beg for more! When I walk, I don't go far. Those few steps are all I need. I get to where I want to be. I bark when I want to go outside. My pet mom picks me up and holds me tight. She holds me up so I don't fall! Good thing I'm not 10 feet tall!

I lost my sight and hearing a while ago. I became scared and couldn't cope. That's when I started to growl and bite. My pet mom tried to comfort me, but soon she became afraid of me. A couple of weeks ago, it was time to let me go, she stayed strong for me I know. Almost 14 years we were together. I loved her so and she loved me. We'll have that special bond forever.

It is amazing how pets can have fun in the midst of their declining days. They seem to know when the time has come when death should have no more delays. They seem to appreciate a master's merciful decision when it is it time to allow the pain ending incision.

While it is a personal decision, deciding to be with their pet in these final moments can be painful but meaningful. One person shared with me that her cat put her head and one paw on her arm when the final moments before the injection came. This person found the time to be precious even though the grief was immeasurable and life was not the same.

Coping with Multiple Losses At Once Complicates Grief Dynamics

Pets can be lost in wildfires, hurricanes, tsunamis, tornadoes, and a myriad of national catastrophes. As a result, one has to deal with multiple losses simultaneously. One may deal with the loss of a pet, family, friends, and their home at once. This kind of grief can be traumatic. Healings journey is heightened and not automatic.

Other Pets in the House Whole May be Grieving from the Loss

How to handle your other pets that were bonded to the pet you lost is a person decision.

There may not be easy answers. One option that may be possible is to show the pet to the other pets. They in some sense can then have some closure. It may not be appropriate if the body was badly injured in an accident. Finding ways to help other pets to grieve can be a creative intuitive venture that fits your personality. It certainly can take energy and add to the challenge of your grief experience.

Unsupportive People May Lecture, Which Can Hurt Instead of Help

A noxious support system can become a liability, heightening the symptoms of grief. As a result, grief can be prolonged, and the natural healing process will take longer for relief. Unsupportive people may lecture, which can hurt and cause grief's healing to retreat.

Saying it was God's will does not focus on what the person is going through regarding the loss. Some people like to gloss over the pain by telling others that God picked a beautiful flower for his garden. More blunt statements can be harmful. Saying "You think you have had it bad. Let me tell you about . . .," keeps the person from being present to the grieving person's pain. Then helping becomes all about the helper and not the person that they are trying to help.

The following statement can shame a person in the midst of their grief's journey's pain: "Why don't you just get another pet?" This question undermines the depth of grief's pain. It could work for some people, but for others, it could be premature and cover up grief's stain. As a result, it could delay grief as it has stifled grief's healing gain. For others, getting another pet may be the answer when the grief is not so intense. For others, they may decide to not obtain another pet as they say it can never be the same. They feel that it would be hard to accept another pet. Also, they may feel that they cannot face another loss yet.

For someone to say simply "I understand" may not be wise. In grief, there may just be some common semblance, but your grief may have a different nuance. Your experience in relation to theirs may not fit. It may feel like they do not understand you a bit. There are elements of your pain that you wish people could understand. You need someone to understand the unique grief symptoms that you experience. When they listen and you know that they care about understanding your particular plight, it can bring in some healing warmth and light. Well-meaning people may strongly confront. They think in a short while you should be more buoyant. Some people respond by becoming more distant. They may be silently sitting in judgment.

Traits of Helpful, Supportive People

Supportive people are fully present. They know that support is greatly needed because grief can be enormously and shockingly unpleasant. The level of the initial, intense pain can seem permanent. Accepting reality can be temporarily absent, and guilt can be annoyingly incessant. Anger can be uncharacteristically poignant. Supportive people are patient but are not abundant.

Recovery, with its challenging adjustments, can be exhausting. Sharp, painful dynamics can feel like the loss is enormously and emotionally costing. The level of the initial intense pain can seem permanent. Therefore, you need someone who is supportive and has wise discernment. They need to encourage you but also allow you to grieve at your own pace. You will feel their patience and not have to race.

People who know how to give support will listen with concern and be fully present. They will grant dignity, and their attitude will be respectful and reverent. They will not lecture with words that come like a torrent. They will provide a presence that you deserve and warrant. They will affirm your dealing with grief and see that you are valiant. By the time that it takes for you to come to terms with grief, they will be patient, wise, and reliant. They will not tell you what to do, like a sergeant or tyrant. They may encourage you to take small steps forward when you are reticent.

They will be by your side in your grief movement. Regarding your strong feelings, they will allow you to vent. In listening, they will be fervent and not flippant. They will sense when to be with you and be silent. They will gradually give you hope that you will again return to being vibrant. This hope will enable your grief journey to be more gallant. They will acknowledge steps forward when you have moments of being effervescent.

Reaching out for support from others during grief can enable one to gradually be pulled back into life. Knowing what can really help you can enable you to seek out a person that will be loyally rife. Receiving support from others can help even in the darkness of the night. Reaching out to others can help one in the midst of darkness to see the light.

A spark of hope and of healing can arise. You then can have grateful feelings of coming back to life, which you can greatly espouse. Networking can change what you thought you could not change, and you are ready to take your healing bows. You can begin a journey of healing that support allows.

You can see the possibilities ahead, and you can begin to lose the daily grief dread. You can find life reemerging instead. You can creatively come out on the other side ahead. Your heart will not feel like it is being shredded. Your purpose, passion, and excellence will increase to a new level. You can use the creative coping skills of grief to change your life that has been disheveled.

Managing Stress Can Prevent Grief from Becoming an Overwhelming Test.

The terrorist attack in September 11, 2001, was chaotic and overwhelming. It was as if the whole nation had been struck with thunder and lightning. This kind of complex, traumatic grief is much more difficult and un inviting. Prominent figures were in hiding after the blast. Heroes kept the White House from experiencing a devastating plane crash. Tears and fears surfaced all over this land, and no one knew if we were going to be attacked again and again.

Over 3,000 people were killed. The mayor of New York had to be strong-willed. Since most people have pets, over 2,000 pets could have grieved over these deaths. This devastating time has put us on alarm because of the continuous terrorist threats. What the future holds regarding the level of danger is impossible to guess. We are experiencing an unknown, dangerous level of stress. When will we be hit again by jets? This is an event that no one forgets.

When will the nuclear bomb for terrorists become more than just a practice test? This unprecedented time helped our country to coalesce. It would be interesting if pet stories around the loss could be published. Traumatic stress is the most challenging disturbance. It takes a community's understanding to help the person traumatized to not fall. With adequate support and inner strength, one can again stand tall. In the meantime, the harrowing experience can overwhelm the mind, body, and spirit. One is left with symptoms that people may say are without merit.

When your mind starts racing and breaks your peaceful, emotional speed limit, it may increase you loss's lament. You need at times to check the speedometer in your mind and see if you are cruising or speeding. It is important to get an accurate odometer's reading. The faster our mind speeds, the more our life becomes a blur. We may become busy and speedy as an escape and not allow grief to occur.

I was seriously injured by a truck driver a few months ago. His mind was speed-messaging his girlfriend, and regarding the gas pedal, he did not even let go. He ran a red light and never took his foot off the gas. While the red light said "Stop," he did not even go slowly.

He crashed into my driver's door, which resulted in a nine-day stay at the hospital. We need to know when to lift our foot off the gas pedal and also when to slow down with the brake. If we don't, we could intensify our emotional wreckage. To deal with this shocking experience, I put my mind on hold so as not to imagine what might be in the package of Pandora's Box. I shut my eyes, and the paramedics cut me out of the car.

I spoke as little as possible to relax to lessen the pain. The process of getting me out of the car resulted in an anguishing, painful jar. I was helped by not allowing my mind to become overwhelmed by the unknown, possible repercussions. I did not know what overwhelming consequences would follow the doctor's discussions.

The wreck was a great intrusion. I was fortunate and completely healed, and the recovery was no illusion. During the time of healing, I found I could upgrade the quality of my writing. It enabled me to slow down and find life more peaceful and exciting.

It is vital that we develop skills of slowing our minds down. If we do not, we may wear a continuous frown. Deep breathing is a universal way of relaxing. Sports figures utilize this method to be able to handle the pressure of a suspenseful game that is emotionally taxing.

When a basketball player gets ready to shoot a free throw, you will often see him or her take a deep breath before their throw to be exacting. We function better when our mind, body, and spirit are relaxing. I often have to remind myself to slow down and cruise in the present moment. Professional golfers typically have one swing thought in a tournament.

In practice, they may have many thoughts. One golfer who won a national amateur tournament at an early age wore a note around her wrist that said, "Do not think of any thoughts." Not letting my mind go wild regarding the potential repercussions of the crash helped me to endure my lungs' gash. I was able to not make decisions that were rash. Life can flow without the clutter of racing thoughts that can cause our mind, body, and spirit to impulsively crash.

No matter what your endeavor or circumstances are, deep breathing can bring out the depths of your coping strengths and talents. Anxiety can create a vicious circle of mental violence. Stress, if unmanaged, can promote shallow breathing, increasing anxiety's negative consequence. Thoughts may come and diminish focused mental practicality. One may not be focused on reality. It takes a conscious intention to breathe more slowly to fully utilize one's mentality.

Robert Trent Jones, a famous golfer who designed The Master's golf course, has been often quoted as saying that the most important aspect about playing golf is what is between your two ears. Follow your heart, but carry your brain with you. Strong emotions and a strong mind together create success in life's game. Then creative attitudes and behavior can keep your mental state soundly sane. Needless emotional debris can be put in the trash, and you can reap the rewards of positive, emotional, and tangible cash.

One way to force oneself to breathe properly is to sit in a chair, bend over, and press the abdomen against the lap. This position forces you to breathe from your diaphragm and receive abundant oxygen to reduce mental gap. When you sit up and speak, you will find that your voice has more resonance and is deeper. You will find that your mind is more alert and able to face challenges that are steeper. You will feel more centered, and regarding grief, you will use a mental sweeper to place in the trash the thoughts that are making your grief pain steeper.

For centuries, monks have used meditation to clear and calm the mind. Meditation involves closing one's eyes and freeing one's mind from feeling imprisoned in penitentiaries. It is, in a spiritual sense, resting in the spirit. It is surrendering and sinking into the source of God's love. Love casts out fear. Love has a calming effect and grants freedom, which is dear.

Of course, if a tiger runs after us, it is okay to have an adrenalin rush.

With needless fear, we may rush our speech when we should hush. Rushing can produce an internal fuss, which can prevent good feelings from disappearing in a flash. We continue the bad feelings through a mental rehash. Coming to a resting place deeply within is rejuvenating. The mind, body, and spirit can be harmoniously resonating.

When we left our mother's womb and entered the world, we felt a jolt. Stress increased as our responsibilities spoke. Even in the womb, the fetus can feel the stress of its mother. The additional stress of having and eat increases life's experiences that may bother. There is no growth without stressful times. Experiencing stress, while moving out of our comfort zone, can be reframed as growing pains. This is healthy, unless the stress is overwhelmingly high, reducing life's gains.

It is a well-known fact that if one takes a baby bird out of the egg without the bird having pecked its way out, it will not have the energy to develop. One needs to stretch one's strength to surround one's lifestyle and completely envelop. Stretching our life's envelope can enable us to write a letter of life with more substance.

Moving out of our comfort zone is the catalyst for growth. Without this risk, we will never experience the adventure of learning a new skill or experience something different. We will stagnate, and our lives will turn sour. Stress can then be our best friend. Stress can catapult us in the adventure of living. It can ignite the unfolding of our lives. The proper amount of stress can help us to operate at the peak of our potential. Embracing stress is a necessary part of effective living.

Too much stress can become a distress. Some hospitals now take babies directly from the womb to a warm water to lessen the transitions stress. The journey from the womb to the world will not feel like such a jolt, and the cry for breath will not be intended as a revolt. The oxygen received will be like a comfortable, energizing, mild electrical volt.

When we are under too much stress, our functioning on all levels is reduced. Our emotions are at war and are yearning for a truce. All of us at times will have more on our plate that we need, resulting in an emotional indigestion. Historically we have minimized trauma's emotional imposition. Understanding the impact of emotional trauma is important in recovery. It sets the foundation for the challenging recovery to result in a creative discovery. The journey toward healing can begin, which is necessary.

It has been only in recent times that we have taken a serious look at understanding emotional trauma. The Vietnam War pushed us to face the horrific symptoms of the post-traumatic stress disorder (PTSD). In the book of Job in the Bible, Job experienced a traumatic experience. At the core of trauma is loss. Job experienced more than grief; it was a complicated, traumatic grief. Job lost his seven sons and three daughters, 7,000 sheep, 3,000 camels, 500 donkeys, and all of his servants, except for a few.

Boils developed from the top of his head to the bottom of his feet. Cumulated traumatic stress overwhelmed his mind, body, and spirit. Job sat in silence for seven days in shock. Then as he began to come out of his shock, these are some of the words that he used to express his anguish. These feelings are not uncommon for someone to temporarily feel after a traumatic experience:

"Let the day perish wherein I was born" (Job 3:3). "Let the blackness of the day terrify it" (Job 3:5). "Why did I not die in the womb?" (Job 3:5) "Oh, that my grief was thoroughly weighed and my calamity laid in the balances together it would be heavier than the sand of the sea" (Job 6:1-3). Bildad the Shihite shamed him and said, "How long wilt thou speak these things and how long shall the words be like a strong wind?" (Job 8:2). Job appropriately replied, "Miserable comforters are ye all" (Job 16:3).

When one is traumatized, one does not need to have one's feelings shamed or discounted. It is important to be able to express them. Job was experiencing normal feelings from an abnormal, overwhelming experience. Job had the safety needs of his family violated. He also had his safety needs threatened as sickness engulfed his body. The safety needs of his servants and family were also violated, creating overwhelming loss.

I had the privilege of interviewing a former Vietnam veteran and with his permission used the information that he shared as part of a research project. Parts of the scenario have been changed for reasons of confidentiality. In his service in the army, he had terrifying experiences that resulted in PTSD responses.

One vivid, memorable incident occurred on Christmas Day when he and his fellow soldiers suddenly experienced a barrage of open fire with bullets penetrating the ground like raindrops. In a futile effort of finding some safety, they immediately jumped into water up to their waist. They were still out in the open at the mercy of the snipers.

For fourteen hours, the bullets pierced the sky over their heads. During this time, they did not know when the rifles would be aimed directly at them. They knew that any second any one of them could be dead. In defense, they shot back in a futile effort as they did not know where the sniper was located.

They did not feel a sense of control. They were in an overwhelming position of striving to accept what they could not change. All of a sudden, the firing mysteriously stopped. It seemed that the sniper was simply toying with them. During those long fourteen hours, the veteran felt that he could die at any moment.

The challenge of accepting what he could not change was not easy in light of the overwhelming, stressful experience. It is normal for a trauma like this to have a lasting impact that is not easily diminished. One may feel needless shame if one does not understand that recovery from such an experience is a journey. It is a gradual experience of healing to come to terms with an enormously terrifying occurrence.

For eight years on Christmas Day, this normally affable, gregarious man's emotions would shut down. He would freeze emotionally and simply go through the motions of the activities of the family gathering. A person experiences symptoms of fight, freeze, or flight. Their inner reactions and resulting behavior need some light for treatment to begin to reduce their confusion and fright.

After having experienced trauma, serenity is very challenging to find. It is not easy to recover one's peace of mind. This response was normal for him to re-experience the terror of that traumatic day. With support and taking care of himself, he gradually began to experience Christmas in a more normal way.

His acceptance of the things that he could not change took a slow but gradual healing process. Having that helpless, death-defying, traumatic fourteen-hour experience was stress that grew over time and overwhelmed his mind, body, and spirit. He had milder symptoms than Job. But he did have times when anger was triggered, when he felt frightened and wanted to escape, and times like on Christmas when he froze.

I asked him how he was able to cope as well as he did. He said that his family taught him a sense of autonomy. In God and in himself he did trust. His autonomy gave him a coping thrust. He became a minister inspiring others in the midst of changes and losses to adjust.

We need to have patience and understanding of others who have had the misfortune of experiencing a traumatic event. Also, we need to have patience with ourselves if a traumatic event has befallen us. The event can come up from time to time and stare one in the face. Flashbacks can be triggered as one relives the shocking scenario. Job's friends were not helpful as they did not understand the affects of trauma stacked upon trauma. The harrowing experience can overwhelm the mind, body, and spirit. They are left with symptoms that people may often say are without merit.

Of course, if a tiger runs after us, it is okay to get an adrenalin rush.

We then can run away from the tiger who wants to make our blood gush. Otherwise, we may rush when we should hush. Rush produces an internal fuss, which creates static in the radio of our lives. Coming to a resting place deeply within ourselves gives us rejuvenating vibes. A calm mind and spirit can become marvelous guides.

When we are under too much stress, our functioning on all levels is reduced. All of us will have more on our plate that we need at one time. A stress level of five helps us to operate at the peak of our potential time after time. A stress level of two would result in a lack of motivation. One may be apathetic. A stress level of seven or eight would begin to make the circumstances overwhelming, and one's functioning would begin deteriorate. A proper level of stress can then be our best friend as it can ignite the unfolding of our lives to mend and begin.

A disastrous death makes the tug boat's challenge great. To get the boat ashore, the boat must tow the extra weight. The tears of the passengers have loaded the ship, which can make it seem like the shore is an impossible trip. Seeing others make it to shore can inspire hope. This inspiration can grant strength needed to cope. As the shore becomes sighted and they see land, the grievers can begin to take command.

It is natural to question God during a time of grief. No answers prevent some anguishing relief.

One's pet may become lost. Why he can't be found can result in profound emotional cost. Well-meaning people can strive to give answers in an effort to divert one's attention away from the painful, grieving goodbye. Comfort comes with another's compassionate presence who understands if you have the need to cry. Gradually, God, who seemed so far away, can then take up residence as a spiritual ally.

One may not need professional help if one is gradually healing. On the other hand, if one becomes stuck in grief or the pain becomes too difficult to bear, finding a therapist who understands grieving from a tragedy can help heal the cracks in one's faith and family. One could easily slip into a clinical depression wherein professional help would be vitally handy.

When I was taking ROTC in college, which is military training, we had a competitive play day. We were divided into teams. The challenge before us was to rotate ten times around the top of a coke bottle with our head on top. Then we were to run to a coke bottle some 150 feet away. Again, we were to rotate ten times and then run back to the first coke bottle.

When it became my turn, I put my head on top of the first bottle and rotated ten times. I was so dizzy I wobbled like an inebriated person to the next coke bottle. I felt an overwhelming challenge as I placed my extremely dizzy head on top of the coke bottle. I was not looking forward to what kind of shape I would be in after the next ten rotations.

I reluctantly completed the ten rotations, and I was so dizzy I fell to the ground. All I could do was get up and steady myself to slowly ramble to the first coke bottle. My functioning increasingly deteriorated under the stress of the circular motions. I was in a severe state of disequilibrium and inner commotion. I was at the opposite state of the continuum of feeling balanced locomotion.

Accepting what cannot be changed helps, but the stress that one absorbs when one experiences a trauma is a different and stressful category. Understanding the magnitude of stress resulting from trauma can help one to have more compassion to oneself and to others who have experienced such a calamity. When trauma wrecks and rocks our soul, we need prayerful support to keep us whole.

Also, you need courage to keep. bold. All of us to some degree experience traumatic reactions. It may be on the lower end of the continuum, but magnifying it by placing it toward the highest level of the continuum helps us in understanding stress on a lesser level. We have experiences that may stick with us. The memory may have a grip on our souls.

The 911 incident still rings in our ears as it echoes from the past. The reverberations from this devastating, emotional earthquake still produce aftershocks and tremors. We are learning as a nation how to deal with trauma, which individuals have been experiencing for many centuries. Learning how to continue our lives amidst a world out of control can be difficult. It is our challenge to learn what we can and cannot change regarding terrorism.

Vietnam and 911 have brought traumatic dynamics to the fore. People understand better how extreme stress can hurt to the core. The symptoms are not easily resolved as they hurt much more. It takes resolve to help the emotions to begin to be healed as one has been hurt to the core. Coping with the most hideous of people is difficult as we expect there will be more gore. This unprecedented rise to power of terrorists is something we deplore. We are going to do all we can to say, "No more."

There is no timeframe for grieving. One never completely heals from death, much less a tragic death. Grief can surface with strong emotions for some time. As one heals, the pain of grief gradually lessens. Tragic grief can leave some indelible impressions. One is asked, "When are you going to get over it?" Grief is a slow process of healing bit by bit. One never completely heals from a deep loss. But when people experience compassion, it is beyond cost. A person can gradually come back into the land of the living when others are understanding and giving.

A tragedy definitely tries the soul, but one can cope and deal creatively with the ordeal. The trial can broaden one's horizon regarding the human plight. The soul may be severely tried, but it can survive and eventually thrive.

Forgiveness: A Wise Choice in Responding to Thorny People

Another factor that can contribute to traumatic grief is if your pet had been intentionally killed. The circumstances surrounding this tragic pet loss complicates pet loss immensely through enormous ill-will. Coping with tragic grief can result in an overwhelmingly emotional shrill.

A difficult person's behavior can sometimes leave a gash, and this infected wound will not quickly dash. Forgiveness can feel insurmountable to begin. Forgiveness can be a process that brings deep healing within. Be patient with yourself. You have many feelings that cannot be put on a shelf.

Forgiveness is a journey in which these strong feelings may take time to begin to melt. Some of these feelings may continue to periodically surface and be felt. If some of the feelings fade, your forgiveness is beginning to be made. Some difficult resentment feelings may be indefinitely delayed. It can bring comfort that some progress is being made.

A person is still held accountable for the consequences of their behavior. If someone shot and killed your loved one, you would not say immediately, "I forgive you. You must have had a bad day." It is similar to the grief process. One has to go through stages in order to come to terms with the damage of the underserved trauma. Otherwise, it would be premature forgiveness and not face the reality of the drama.

Growing from Despair to Creative Coping Skills Repair

Grief is unpleasant. The level of the initial, intense pain can seem permanent. Accepting reality can be temporarily absent. Guilt can be annoyingly incessant. Anger can be uncharacteristically poignant. How people minimize your experience can seem like an affront. Some people in response to your grief may be insensitively blunt.

Grief is complicated with past and present stresses. As a result, you need to creatively cope when the pain is at its crest. You need to gain more support than what is typically needed to cope with grief at your best. Patience can help you endure the time it takes before you recover your zest. Increased coping skills have been spawned by your creative grief journey's quest.

During the anguishing journey of grief, you have experienced added coping skills. These coping skills can empower you to surge toward greater conditions. Enhanced coping skills have given your emotions greater nutrition. You have been strengthened to envision greater life intentions. The mission and vision serve as your life's new inventions. Your resulting, clearer values can result in sound decisions. You can now move from grief to the greatness that you envision. Moving toward purpose, passion, and excellence can result in much fruition. The pain of your grief can experience attrition.

You will have been empowered to overcome opposition. Others will see your life differently as you are on a creative expedition. They will clearly give you genuine recognition. You can become free from any inhibition. Each choice will become your future's voice. The direction of your life from grief to greatness can cause reason for you to rejoice.

Your life can be like poetry in motion instead of chaotic, inharmonious commotion. When you go toe to toe with life, you will face challenges with a new sense of might. Obstacles will try to make you think you cannot deal with life as it is. They can jump out of nowhere like a pop quiz. Your strengthened coping skills will enable you to face what is actual. You will not have to change the reality of what is factual. You are on your journey toward excellence, purpose, and passion. You can handle life in an outstanding fashion.

PART 2

GROWING FROM GRIEF
TO GREATNESS

CHAPTER 5

Creatively Facing the
Reality of Change

Without facing reality, your life may be wayward.
Facing reality is important in helping you to focus and move forward.

—Dan Crenshaw

FACING REALITY IS paramount in dealing with grief as well as effectively coping with life. Dealing with the reality of change is at the heart of pet loss. In grief, you have the challenge of realistically accepting what you cannot change and change what you can. Change, transition, and letting go were a part of the grief dynamics in part one. Dealing realistically with change issues is also at the heart of a purposeful life. This chapter elaborates on change issues and coaches you how to navigate change in your whole lifestyle.

The Serenity Prayer is a good resource in dealing realistically with change mattes. Changing what you can change is empowerment. Accepting what you cannot change is letting go. Wisdom, serenity, and courage are traits needed to maneuver through your transition. These coping traits can contribute to your moving toward your passion, purpose, and excellence. You can grow creatively from grief to greatness.

Accepting what you cannot change can set you free. Changing what you can change can help you see that life has a larger possibility. Living in transition can seem like a mean time. The Serenity Prayer can help it to become a meaningful time. You can face reality and creatively reach your prime. You can find limbs on your tree of life to climb.

The famous Serenity Prayer is as follows:

God, give us grace to accept with serenity the things that cannot be changed, courage to change the things that should be changed, and the wisdom to distinguish the one from the other. (*The Serenity Prayer: Faith and Politics in Times of Peace and War* [Elisabeth Sifton W. W. Norton, October 2003, p. 277] quotes this version as the authentic original.)

Accepting what we cannot change and changing what we can is a universal yearning. As a result, this prayer has been translated in many languages and is used by millions of people. There is not a day that goes by that we do not encounter unchangeable circumstances. Oftentimes, these events result in internal strife. These states of affairs can include exasperating, annoying occurrences like a traffic jam, which may leave one disgruntled. Furthermore, the situation can be an anguishing struggle resulting from a devastating tragedy. These scenarios, if unattended, can block our view of the future.

They can affect your live for a day or linger for a lifetime. Not coming to terms with what we cannot change can have a crippling effect on our ability to change what we can. What we cannot change can capture us and hold us captive. On the other hand, as we become captivated by the Serenity Prayer, we can be set free from being held hostage. We can become a gracious host inviting the future to become our guest. By being hospitable toward the future, we can provide hospitality to all the opportunities that grace our place.

As a result, the attitudes that we have, the behaviors that we demonstrate, and our emotional state are all at stake. The Serenity Prayer can positively affect these crucial aspects of living, resulting in life tasting like a steak. Accordingly, our whole demeanor and lifestyle depend upon how effectively we handle these issues. The legacy that we leave and our life's footprints are inextricably intertwined in the dynamics of this impactful prayer. For this reason, the Serenity Prayer is perhaps the most universally well-known prayer.

I certainly have spent my share of placing futile energies pondering or regretting what I could not change. The negative impact that this attitude has had upon my life is significant. This prayer has loosened the grip of unchangeable scenarios that have surfaced in my life. As a result, I have more energy to live more creatively in changing what I can.

We simply cannot control everything. It can be a relief to give up the burden of hanging on to that desire or regret. This relief can gradually bring priceless serenity, increasing our quality of life. "Learning how to accept what we cannot change" is perhaps this prayer's most popular use. This book explores this crucial life skill. It also peers beneath the second statement regarding changing what one can. One is beckoned to decide if one is changing what one can in the right manner. Does the end justify the means?

Additionally, the second aspect of the prayer can help one explore if one is striving to make appropriate changes. One may be placing energies in matters that are changeable, but they are matters that are not fitting for one's involvement. One's energies can be better utilized and more suitably in other, more proper endeavors.

One can also learn to distinguish between what is changeable and what is unchangeable. Learning to one's delight that what was previously thought to be unchangeable is in actuality changeable is a powerful accomplishment. This priceless attitudinal and behavioral change is briefly but personally exemplified in the dedication of this book.

All of the juices can be squeezed out of the orange of life as we more effectively incorporate this transforming prayer. As we become engrossed in this prayer, life can be lived at a more optimal level. This empowering prayer can be the optical lenses through which life's perspectives can zoom to new heights. With serenity, wisdom, and courage. Our outlook will be on the lookout for innovative ways to apply this prayer to our behaviors, feelings, and thoughts.

What a purposeful, peaceful life experience we would have if we gazed at life through the eyes of the magnificent Serenity Prayer! Our eyes would twinkle like the stars in the night. With a tranquil glow, we would brighten the lives of the people in our sight. We can come out of darkness into light. Along the way, we can carry others with us to ours and their delight. The Serenity Prayer provides meaning and purpose and helps us to live life overflowing with a peaceful surplus.

Serenity, wisdom, and courage would come together in concert producing symphonic harmony. These three virtues would serve as a tripod, triumphantly supporting the music in our lives. This foundational tripod would then result in life becoming music to our ears. The discord in our behavior, thoughts, and feelings would be diminished.

Then we will be able to set harmony to our lives and live to a symphonic finish. Our lives will sparkle like wood with a coat of varnish. We will not feel like our lives will tarnish. Changing what we can will make our life more colorfully garnished. Others can see the change in your life, and their own lives will be inspirationally embellished.

As the Serenity Prayer becomes a lifestyle, it will fill up our cups until they overflow. This prayer will continuously give us spiritual nourishment. We will "pray without ceasing" (1 Thessalonians 5:17) as the prayer becomes our habitual attitude and outlook. When the goose laid the golden egg, it had to be the Serenity Prayer. It is a treasure beyond measure. Beneath the surface of the prayer are many golden, priceless thoughts that can be mined. The Serenity Prayer can give us the Midas touch, which can result in continuous golden moments that can inspire us so much.

The Serenity Prayer can also become a lighthouse--a beacon leading the ships of our lives toward their proper destination. Your life's ship will not become bogged down or mired in shallow waters or be smashed against a jagged rock. The ship of your life can find direction and come home to dock.

You can avoid a way of destruction, resulting in escaping an avoidable disruption. The Serenity Prayer can produce in our lives a shift that can prevent us from becoming adrift. These words can prayerfully provide a sanctuary of protection, as they help channel your energies in a focused direction. Your life can continually shift and make a needed correction as you avoid self-deception. Furthermore, these choice prayerful thirty-three words can smooth out our sharp edges and grant us more protection.

Emotional, spiky, throbbing wounds that life inevitably brings can experience healing. No longer will there be an anguishing feeling. The pain will be yielding. The lessening of pain can be refreshing. This powerful prayer can become your center of gravity, anchoring and helping you overcome grave situations without derailing. You will stare life in the face without reeling or squealing. The way you deal with difficulties of others will be inspirational and appealing. You do not have to be unfeeling and stoic. You can be emotionally heroic. Strength is being able to share what you have felt with the cards you have been dealt. You can stand on your feet with stamina and emotional health.

The second jewel in this prayer, "changing what we can," provides wisdom to enlighten your path. Then there can be creative rewards in the grief's healing aftermath. By creatively dealing with pain, you will never be the same. Your sense that you can overcome will always remain. You will be empowered to have free reign in life's terrain. Your deep loss has given you a depth of gain. You accepted and let go what you could not change and changed what you could change. Greater possibilities are now in range.

If we are not serene, we may easily be thrown off- balance in life's daunting experiences. The Serenity Prayer wraps it's comforting arms around our lives and helps us gain a healthy life focus. As a result, we can become centered and will not feel a sense of chaotic, emotional ruckus. Your life can be awakened. Your mission and vision will not be forsaken. Serenity, wisdom, and courage can keep you in sync. This prayer can keep you from living on the brink. You will be less apt to sink.

When we accept what we cannot change, our minds will be filled with less clutter. What can be changed is what our minds will powerfully utter. We will become occupied with what we can alter. Being empowered, we have great potential not to falter.

Several years ago I was a director of a counseling center that was a satellite office of a hospital's counseling department. Because of a financial crisis, I was part of a massive employee layoff. My career thereafter was not as fulfilling. To fill the void, I became engrossed with writing. My first venture involved being accepted to write weekly articles for three newspapers.

This experience helped me realize how much I enjoyed writing. My next venture involved writing my first book, which has led to writing this book. My passion for writing was not forsaken. This creative writing passion was awakened. I have now vaulted over the bar into a new creative direction. I am an author and author and poet with passion and affection.

This prayer can help us accept what we want to change but cannot without blaring out a rave and a rant. Then we can have the energy to change what we can and experience the momentum of moving toward our promise land. It can take some time to make significant progress toward our pinnacle. The Serenity Prayer can make our journey enjoyable and not cynical.

As a result, the Serenity Prayer can help us move with and not against the grain of life. The traits of serenity, wisdom, and courage can become life-savoring fruits. Serenity can give us the calmness and patience to let go and let God and flow. Courage can provide us the will to risk when we are out of our comfort zone. Wisdom can grant us the direction that we need to be going on. Then we can be on a journey where we belong.

Next are thoughts on serenity, wisdom, and courage to help cultivate a more receptive mindset as we explore some of the attitudinal applications of this extraordinary prayer. As we consider a serene role model, Gandhi may come to mind. With a serene mind that birthed courage and wisdom, he became an astounding change agent. Thus, he had a huge impact with his peaceful, nonviolent approach. He worked for civil rights from within. Also, he labored to free India from the tyranny of the British colonial authority that had them pinned in.

Without wisdom is to be like a ship without a rudder. Lacking understanding is like living with a continuous shudder. With insight, one can make healthy choices. With good judgment, one can discern the truth in the midst of many voices. Wisdom can be cultivated, as the mind is serene and has become activated in one's life's creative scheme.

As we think of a wise man, King Solomon may come to mind. He displayed enormous wisdom as a judge regarding two women who both claimed that a baby was theirs. One baby died in the night, and both women declared that the living infant was theirs. The king ordered one of his men to obtain a sword. Then he commanded that the child be cut in half and a portion be given to each woman.

The authentic mother pleaded for her child's life by asking that the infant be given to the other woman. The lying lady demanded that the infant be severed in two halves. Solomon then commanded that the child be given to the first woman. Through his wisdom, he set up a situation where the cream rose to the top. The bona fide mother surfaced. Then, the wisdom of Solomon began to spread throughout the land (1 Kings 3:1-28).

Having no courage to cope is like being stuck. Lacking bravery is being like a sitting duck. With valor, one can carry out the changes that one needs to make. These changes are for goodness' sake. We admire people who are extraordinarily courageous. Their display of boldness in the midst of risks is quite contagious. When we pray for courage, we need inspiration to carry out our challenges with undue desperation.

President Roosevelt displayed courage during WWII when he said perhaps his most famous words, "We have nothing to fear but fear itself." He provided great leadership during one of the most challenging times in the history of our country.

Serenity, wisdom, and courage combined can empower us to be emotionally and spiritually agile. Then we can make the needed adjustments to surge toward our potential without being too fragile. Our lives will become dynamically inclined as we stop placing energy on limitations and start placing vigor on our possibilities.

By using the resource of the Serenity Prayer, we may take dead aim in reaching our goals. With composed concentration, our dreams can come to life, originating deeply within our souls. This classical prayer can be inspirational in helping us to step up to the plate and hit the ball in fair territory. We will not be as apt to run afoul. Our lives will become more purposeful and productive.

Consequently, there are a myriad of control ramifications in the tapestry of life. Control issues can be like a thread, giving unity to one's delight. Focusing on what we cannot control can lead us to fright. Consequently, the wrong attitude regarding control can make one feel frayed and threadbare, with no delight.

It is appropriate, then, that this prayer is called the Serenity Prayer because one has no foundation for courage or wisdom without being at ease. Staying unruffled makes life flow like a gentle spring breeze. With the attitude of "easy does it," we can keep a reserve of energy to preserve serenity.

If we try too hard with an exorbitant amount of stress, it may be a signal to stop, look, and listen. With courage, one can gain a strong ambition. Then one can envision one's mission, as it will glisten. As a change agent, one will then be able to fulfill one's purpose, resulting in abundant fruition.

When I was a child, I watched my neighbor cut chickens' heads off in preparation for the family meal. After the heads were cut off, the chickens would run around in circles for many minutes. As our minds are racing and we are trying too hard, we may run in circles, accomplishing very little. We will not be able to effectively use our heads. In a sense, our heads may be off, resulting in our heading in the wrong direction.

An unquiet mind disturbs the soul. This disturbance can make life taste like mold. A quiet mind can live in the present and be powerfully bold. After the grief experience has greatly healed, serenity can be sealed deeply within your soul.

It is normal to feel a state of turmoil when healing has not taken place and adjustments have not been made. Accepting what cannot be changed may not come quickly in totality, but the rays of peaceful sunshine can begin to break through the dark clouds and result in vitality. Then one is on the way through a transition toward adaptability. This transition can result in a growing tranquility. Moving through the time of change can enhance creative mobility.

Coping Creatively with Change Matters: Getting Out of Your Own Way

Accepting what you cannot change and changing what you can help you to get out of your own way. You will gain focus, which can prevent self-defeating ruckus. By getting out of your own way, your continued growth will be here to stay. Coping with grief is enhanced by becoming your own best friend, and you will not betray. As you care for yourself, coping with grief can provide healing within. Moving from grief to greatness will be natural to begin.

Growth is natural for all living things under the right conditions. Having yourself in your own corner will bring ambitions free from inhibitions. You can feel your own power as it becomes your friend. It is power that is good for you and others, resulting in a win-win. Getting out of your own way can become the onset of peace within. You know that you deserve success, and you cannot wait to begin.

You will attract others with your positive energy. Like a rolling snowball, your momentum will accelerate with resulting synergy. Frosty the Snowman will go over the hills of snow. The journey will expand your vision, and you will be in the know. Wisdom, serenity, and courage will continue to grow. You can celebrate your creative life like a beautiful singing bird. The results can reap rewards that go beyond any word.

The expression on your face leaves no doubt regarding your inner passion. You will not feel that your creative energies will have to be under ration. Your bountiful energy will be set free in a multicolored fashion. Then creativity will result from a remarkably efficient action. Any opposition will not result in a retraction. Passion can fuel your life to move through obstacles and can prevent you from experiencing debacles. Negativity will not let the air out of the tires. Your sound attitude will continue life's passionate, burning fires.

CHAPTER 6

Attitudinal Coping Skills

Without a good attitude, a crucial part of growth is missing.
Your attitude is central in gaining a grip on productive living.
Facing reality and letting go can spawn a good attitude.
A good attitude can increase your life's latitude.

—Dan Crenshaw

ATTITUDINAL COPING SKILLS can serve as an umbrella, keeping the rain from drowning out other life skills. Attitudinal coping skills are greatly tested in grief and can become very testy. You can strengthen your attitude during grief by strengthening autonomy as well as reaching out for support. You can use the enhanced attitudinal coping skills that have been nourished.

Attitude is the fertilizer that helps behavioral, emotional, and relational coping skills to flourish. You will not play possum. You can grow toward purpose, passion, and excellence that is awesome. Attitude links the other coping skills together to enable you to powerfully move forward. These coping skills can then work in tandem to help your life not to go wayward.

Being Hopeful Is One of the Most Important Attitudinal Coping Skills

Perhaps the most important attitude is being hopeful. Hope keeps sunshine in sight whether in the darkness or in the light. Hope is the spark of life. Hope broadens your scope. Believing that a goal is possible is the heartbeat of your destiny. This hope is fertilized by wise scrutiny. Hope is the tool to mine jewels from the mind. It enables you to move forward when you feel temporarily blind.

Hope, then, is the light to give sight to one's plight. Hope generates explorative action when the answers to reaching your goal are not clear. Hope is the drive that overcomes obstacles that get in the way of what is dear. Hope is the energy that sustains the exploration to find the way that will result in your goals becoming near. Hope instills in the mind a reason to go on without undue fear.

Pet bonding brings to many people's lives enhanced purpose and hope. It can seem that the tough times in life bring less perspiration by your pet's inspiration. Through the bond with your pet, the thirst for meaning will be significantly quenched. As grief has experienced healing, then hope will not be benched. The spirit of the memories of your pet can keep hope from being lynched. Inspiration can be enhanced, and you can have a hopeful dance. You will not become stuck in desperations' trance.

Hope as the fertilizer will provide vitality to help you advance. The importance of hope in dealing with pet loss was mentioned in the first chapter. It is significant to revisit and expand some of these ideas to help hope loom large in your entire outlook on life. The seeds of hope can be planted within you from unexpected places.

Hope was fertilized by your relationship with your pet. The challenge of regaining a higher level of hope and purpose looms large as your pet is missed. You have to move through a time when purpose and hope seem not to clearly exist. Now you need to boost your sense of hope from other newly found places to give your outlook a positive twist and enable you to persist.

Hope Can Turn Frustration into Fruits

Frustration can drain your energy dry. There is more to frustration that meets the eye. When you become stuck in frustration, you lose your power. You can become weaker every hour. You may see the obstacle as something that you cannot overcome. You wish you could find a way, but your brain stays mum. Hope can help you to see your situation in a new light. You can move forward with direction and sight. You can turn frustration into fruits of your labor. Playing big can help you to be unstoppable and to never waver.

You can find power to carve out a path that will overcome the obstacles aftermath. You can find increasing energy to use to surge forward. With each step, your confidence will be bolstered. As hope turns frustration into fruits, there can be attitudinal nutrients in the tree of your life's roots.

Humor is a vitamin that can help you see life's experiences it a more dignified instead of demeaning manner. Humor can help you transform the situation and turn frustration into a delightful encounter. In the first section of this book, I told the following scenario in a manner that left me feeling demeaned.

The following version of the scenario has been revised to incorporate humor and make it more palatable and delightfully laughable:

You are about to experience a stunning, super heroic scenario. This nonstop, gripping escapade will keep you clinging to the edge of your seats. I invite you to absorb unforeseen gallantry in the midst of insurmountable odds. The only way that I can help you capture even a glimpse of the level of heroism that I displayed is to be . . . Superman! I ripped off my regular shirt and proudly revealed my Superman T-shirt. Before I embark on this scenario, it is vital for me to warn you that this dramatic event has received the new rating *PR*, which stands for *Perfectly Ridiculous*.

Now, allow yourself to become *entrenched* in this *breath-taking* scene. It is a military environment. The ROTC students at Clemson University were asked to successfully execute the impossible, but I reminded myself that I was Superman. We were lined up into groups of ten. Two containers were placed in front of each team a *dazzling* 100 feet apart.

The instructor had the audacity to order each person on each team to take turns, bend down, and place their foreheads squarely on the mouth of the first bottle and turn around ten times. Then, we were further ordered to run in a straight line 100 feet to the second bottle.

To make the physical feat even more astronomical, at the second container we were commanded to repeat the ten gigantic gyrations all over again. As Superman, naturally, I was unanimously elected to be the powerful leader of our team.

When the gun fired to start the race, I felt a bullet of fear strike my heart. Reality brutally *bombarded* my brain and reminded me that I have motion sickness, but I reminded my mind that I was . . . Superman.

I gathered my wit and undauntedly bent over and placed my forehead securely on top of the mouth of the first container. Around and around I went, totally oblivious to the devastating repercussions these perilous maneuvers were going to inflict. When I completed my tenth circular movement, I arose not composed. I was far more unstable than a severely intoxicated man. But I reminded myself that I was Superman. I heroically staggered toward the goal of reaching the second container 100 dazzling feet away. Being extraordinarily dizzy and unstable, I weaved back and forth, crisscrossing the straight line.

Second Bottle

I now stood above the second bottle, overwhelmed at executing the upcoming impossible task. In fact, I felt like I would rather be executed. I knew that going around ten more times under this dire duress would render me totally and traumatically dysfunctional. To make matters worse, in the midst of the whirling of my mind, the container became a circling, moving target! I attempted to place my forehead squarely down on the mouth of the bottle and completely missed. Then, with uncommon determination, my head miraculously found its destination on my fifth superhuman heroic effort.

After my tenth circle around the bottle, dizziness engulfed me. I became much more than tipsy. As a result, I tipped over and fell flat and face-first on the ground with an enormous thud. Some lunatics yelled that I was a dud. I idiomatically bit the dust, but literally I bit the dirt. Panicking, my breathing escalated. Poor, helpless dirt was sucked down my throat and lodged there. It did not feel like I or the dirt were like lodging in a hotel. It felt like we were in, well . . . hell.

To make matters even more catastrophic, there was little room for air to travel through my throat. As a result, inadequate oxygen reached my brain. I was left with far less than half a brain. I tried desperately to remember that I was Superman. With phenomenal heroism, I marched toward my dire destiny.

Step by step, I began to fulfill the outrageous objective of returning to the first container, which was the finish line, 100 treacherous feet away. Halfway there, under the enormous weight of my dizziness, my knees buckled again. I plunged to the ground with such enormous force that my teeth became embedded three inches into the dirty dirt. My breathing became even more rapid. Even more dirt was lodged into my windpipe. Consequently, the fact that I would finish the race alive seemed like a pipedream.

There was virtually no space for oxygen to pass through my throat. I gagged, but this was no gag. It was perilously serious. It was a breath-taking drama. My breath was virtually taken away. My dizziness zoomed. I felt doomed. I was now operating on only 10 percent of my brain's capacity. But with phenomenal effort, I remembered that I was Superman. Therefore, in the midst of incredibly insurmountable odds, I reached my final destination. Then, the dirt lunged from my throat to its freedom. I was no longer breathless.

My team experienced the red badge of embarrassment. Then they all broke out into uncontrollable laughter. This empowering laughter became a potent medicine. Laughter ignited my team to victory without any reticence. Our empowered team defied predictability. I was carried off the field on my team's shoulders as a hero, but my team could not stop laughing.

May laughter never stop being your powerful ally. When it seems like you are going in calamitous circles, you will not fall and bite the dust. You will march confidently forward and obtain and share life's golden dust.

Overcoming Denial Responsibly: A Vital Life-Coping Skill

Overcoming denial and facing reality is not only vital in grief, but it is also invaluable for the quality of your lifestyle. In grief, it is vital that we do not get stuck in denial. If we remain stuck in denial of the important aspects of life, our movement toward purpose, passion, and excellence can be on trial. Denial is a common defense mechanism regarding addictions and an array of life's multifaceted issues.

All of us have blind spots. For one reason, we cannot or will not face reality. It is our responsibility to face reality and wisely respond to what shows up in our lives with vitality. Facing reality can transform one's life in totality. We can respect the reality of our limitations through accepting what we cannot change. As a result, we can focus our energy and surge toward our possibilities by changing what we can.

There are other ways of denial. One might say, "I do not have an anger problem. It is you that causes me to be angry. I do not have a control issue." These denials can have a devastating effect on relationships. Denial can result in a huge defense mechanism. This defense prevents people from learning about themselves and their learning curves. This denial can result in a person running off the road of life's curves with uncontrolled swerves. Not seeing one's shortcomings can result in one's many blunderings that can rattle one's comings and goings.

By using denial temporarily prevents one from being overwhelmed by a traumatic situation. By gradually facing reality, a person can see the challenges that need to be overcome. If reality is continually blurred, one may be surprised what detrimental consequences may occur.

Many people do not face reality regarding health issues and how best to prevent and catch medical issues early. I had a valve replacement ten years ago, and my heart is operating normally. One man denied the need to see a doctor, and his heart murmur went undetected and was undiagnosed.

Tracking when the timing for surgery should be done went lacking. When he did go to a doctor, his increasingly poor functioning heart valve overworked his heart so badly that they could not fit a new valve as a replacement. His overworked heart had enlarged, making the challenge of replacing the valve too large. He did not live much longer.

Facing reality is important for us to maximize our potential mentally, emotionally, and physically. The coping skills that help one to navigate one's life through grief can help one to grow toward purpose, passion, and excellence. Denying real guilt or denying that we are demeaning ourselves with false guilt are both self-defeating. Being perfectly imperfect is worth repeating, as it applies not only to grief but also to your whole lifestyle.

As a result of strengthening your attitudinal coping skills, you can increase your mental, emotional, and spiritual will. You can become much savvier in dealing with life with wisdom being instilled. With a good attitude, you will be able to climb when life is uphill. With a good attitude regarding your goals, you will be fulfilled.

CHAPTER 7

Relational Coping Strategies

A healthy relationship with yourself is foundational for a solid life stance.
Then your relationship with others can blossom and your life can advance.
Relational coping skills are needed in grief.
You need to relate well toward yourself and others to gain relief.
In your whole lifestyle, relational coping strategies
can maximize your possibilities.
As a result, you can discover more of your potential and abilities.

—Dan Crenshaw

Autonomy Can Provide an Anchor.

AUTONOMY WAS ADDRESSED in chapter 1 relating to coping with pet loss. It is given a different twist here as it moves from grief to empower you to grow towards greatness. Autonomy is your relationship with yourself. It is a foundation to relate healthily to others. A sense of independence is expanded in this section to help strengthen your fulfillment. To have a healthy sense of independence can be foundational for interdependence.

Consequently, your life will be enhanced by receiving and giving to others without being needy or greedy. You will be generous instead of onerous. In grief work, one needs to grieve independently by oneself. Also, you need to network with a system of support. Support helps to give the energy to grieve. Autonomy and support can converge for powerful coping to surge.

Autonomy is a lifetime developmental process. A two-year-old will say, "Mommy, I'll do it myself." A two-year-old will say, "No! No! No!" It is the first step in a child's life to gain a sense of his or her own power. This can be a draining stage for a parent. The need for this fledgling skill to develop is apparent. It is important for each person to gain a sense of independence. It enables one to cope with life that makes much sense.

Teenagers have a wave of energy regarding exploring their potency to impact their lives. Their energies need to be harnessed. As they bump up against authority, they can learn from their lumps. They can learn to skillfully harness their energies in a manner that is untarnished. They can develop a balance of independence and teamwork that will enable their lives to shine like having a coat of varnish.

Stubbornness is Autonomy Gone Wild.

To be too independent is to be stubbornly unyielding. This rigidity is an unhealthy attitude toward yourself and results in an unhealthy relationship with others that is not appealing. One can be relentlessly unbending in their limited view. The clouds of fog will result in wise judgments being all too few. Your life's direction can become askew. Stubbornness has too much traction, producing friction which can hinder cooperative, dynamic interaction.

On the other hand, being an independent thinker can spawn creativity. Being a stubborn thinker can result in defensiveness and reactivity. By being stubborn, one cannot reach out for help. One does not understand the difference receiving support has made in how others felt. By being stubborn, one cannot cooperate with a team. One does not know what "two heads are better than one" can mean.

By being stubborn, one can often be rude. One can be so independent that one will not be able to relate and learn from others. If an illness is stubborn, it will not heal. A person who is bullheaded will not yield, heal, or grow toward a purpose to fulfill. A bull in a fight is headed in the wrong direction. Being attracted to the red color results in its becoming bloody red.

A driver in a car that will not yield can have a wreck. A stubborn person can then go their own way without a speck of wisdom. A stubborn person can go through life in an arrogant prison. A hardheaded person can have boundaries that are too strong. They will not let others into telling them when they are wrong. They will not be perfectly imperfect; they will be imperfectly imperfect.

Being stubborn can make one not be able to say, "I am sorry." They are self-centered and want all of the glory. They will not know when they make others realistically worry. Being stubborn inhibits one from reaching one's potential. They do not realize that learning from others to grow is essential.

Being wisely independent can help you to be strong and not surrender. You may learn from others, but you will know when others hinder. You can be a unique, creative thinker. You can have a willingness to not go along with the crowd and always do what others may expect. This independent wisdom can help you to have passion, purpose, and excellence that others may eventually respect.

Conversely, being overly autonomous and independent regarding grief and life can hamper healing and growing. It is crucial to allow times for receiving. There are times that we need to be on the receiving end. A life of giving and receiving makes for a fulfilling blend.

Balancing Autonomy with Receptivity

Being on the receiving end helps you to network. It keeps one from wasting time doing too much needless guesswork. A network is a place for leadership and learning. Networking comes from a purposeful yearning. The more people you know, the more success you will be earning. Possibilities can open up that can lead one down an exciting path. Putting heads together can prevent power struggling wrath. Teamwork can bring creative serenity and prevent a warpath.

Someone suggested that I become a life coach. They gave me a direction down a previously unknown business to approach. Many people told me that I was a good writer. I began to expand this skill. When we have people believing in us, we can be inspired to change what we previously thought we could not change.

Operating in a vacuum can leave potential untapped. The naysayers can be demeaning and keep you from dreaming. A support system can give your efforts direction and meaning. Your lives with momentum can keep on streaming. A stream is always flowing and moving. With a supportive network, you can find yourself moving toward excellent zooming.

We can cultivate that belief in ourselves that can overcome obstacles. We will not see what is surmountable as insurmountable. We will gain the wisdom to distinguish between the two. The musical instruments of our lives will be in tune with what is changeable and what is possible.

When we are tone-deaf, we do not know when our lives are out of tune. We may be playing notes in our lives that are not in tune with who we are. When we get in tune then our lives can become a creative musical instrument as we become instrumental. As a result, we can live life with purpose, passion, and excellence, which can become monumental.

We need to tune out the false prophets and tune in to the truth. The truth can give us the belief and faith in ourselves that will move mountains. The vistas of life become prettier the further one climbs. Regarding purpose, passion, and excellence, others can help empower us to ring our chimes.

When someone says that it cannot be done, one must not be stunned. Their feedback may be something to be considered, but it is not something necessary to make one reconsider. We must not obsess over what the naysayers say. If we take them too seriously, we may not find our creative way. In any challenge that we encounter, we will handle it better with a support system. This support has the possibility of increasing our wisdom.

If we go it alone, we will miss the boat in what we may change, and we may not be getting genuine feedback when we are barking up the wrong tree. We need to be careful who we place in our support system. We do not need yes people. But at the same time, we do not need negative people. We need wise people to help us gather information to make the best decision possible.

Birth Order Can Influence Assets and Liabilities in Balancing Autonomy.

Birth order may provide different challenges. A first-born child can become overly responsible and not learn to delegate. It may lead to a burden of stress and heartache. By learning how to delegate, a first-born child can often become a great leader. He has a balanced life of integrity and responsibility and is not a fibber.

A second-born child can feel lost in the middle. They can be cantankerous to get attention and their actions become a riddle. Their strength is that they can learn to be a mediator, negotiator, and diplomat. Being caught in the middle, they learn to compromise instead of having an escalating, reactive spat. They can bring a large conflict down to size. Their exceptional skills can bring resolution that can be a pleasant surprise.

A younger child tends to be given more. Less is expected of them, which can make their older siblings sore. They tend to be more playful and relaxed. They have a tendency to make friends easily without being emotionally taxed. They can function in an environment that is productive when they can put people at ease. Then they can influence others without an intimidating squeeze.

You can magnify your efforts by looking to others for help. Then you can change what you can without giving a yelp. Your life will become much stronger when you share the task. Without help, we would never last. By networking, we can be like the train that said it could, and we can become empowered to "choo choo" until we arrive where we should.

Receiving Can Enable You to Discover That You Can Change What Was Unchangeable.

Years ago when I used the YMCA for exercise, I usually used the jogging track and the swimming pool. One occasion, I saw a stationary bike when I passed the weight room. Normally, I would have passed it up. This time I decided to use the stationery bike. As I entered the weight room, I saw a person who had been bench-pressing heavy weights. I looked at him, and to my alarm, he was stuck as he had the weights just above his neck.

He was too exhausted to push the weights above him and set them in the rack. He was helplessly hanging on for dear life as he was continuing to lose energy. It would not have been long until exhaustion would set in, and he could no longer hold the bar above his neck. As a result, the heavy bar with weights on each side was on the brink of beginning its descent upon his neck.

I went over to him and both of us raised the bar above him and put it in the slot. He was helpless by himself, but with my help, he reached his goal. We can feel helpless by ourselves and feel like we have to accept what we cannot change. But with other people's help, there may be some creative answer to the challenge that is waiting to be found.

There is a story that has been circulating around that is well worth repeating. A man was on top of his house and a flood was engulfing his house. He prayed, "Lord, get me out of this situation." A helicopter came over and dropped down a ladder. The man was still praying, "Lord, help me get out of here."

The helicopter could not wait any longer and went to help others. Then a boat arrived and a ladder came out of the boar and stretched to the roof. After a while, it had to leave to help others who would take advantage of the way to escape. The man was very angry at God. "Why don't you help me?" He said. "I sent you a helicopter and a boat."

Mountain climbers go in groups. They help each other. They become a team, which helps each individual reach the summit. If we do not connect with others, we can make a mountain out of a molehill. Life will be harder than it has to be. The obstacles will be magnified to proportions that are beyond reality.

There have been virtually no people that have accomplished things without help outside themselves. Any sports figure will give thanks to many people who help them to hone their skills. Great artists will report that they were influenced by many other artists that came before them or were there contemporaries. Even Shakespeare was influenced by writers that preceded him. Creativity often does not create something new. It builds upon knowledge gained before. If we are not open to being influenced or helped by other people, we may miss the boat.

Information may be constructive criticism that can become the turning point in our accomplishing something that previously felt impossible. The impossible can become possible. The things that we cannot change can be changed. We do need wisdom to know if there is a key that will unlock the door or if we need to realize that as one door closes, there is another one that will open.

The "I'll do it myself" attitude is not always the best formula for success. The people who built a life out west in the days of the frontier were admired for their independent self-sufficiency. Society grows faster when people and cultures link together to share information. Cultures stagnate when there is no history to build upon and knowledge becomes lost. This dynamic led to the Dark Ages in history, and not building upon the knowledge of other can lead us toward years of darkness. The gentleman, who was lifting weights by himself, was becoming closer and closer to darkness. It was fortunate that I happened to enter that room for the first time.

The age of enlightenment was ignited by people linking together to form a chain of events that culminated in the blossoming of knowledge. Self-sufficiency is carried too far when we do not look outside ourselves to see how we can improve by rubbing shoulders with others. The Panama Canal would have never been built if hundreds of people had not worked together to the hilt.

Autonomy: Dealing with Difficult People

In grief, you may deal with people who do harm instead of help. Difficult people are here to stay. In grief and in life, we might as well find a coping way. While in grief, it is highly likely that you have dealt with people that were difficult as they tried to tell you that you should not feel the way that you do and you should get over it quicker.

In life, we have situations where people do not understand our feelings or behavior. This can happen during pet loss and many other aspects of life. This section expands dealing with difficult people to allow it to become a part of your whole lifestyle. Utilizing autonomy to help you deal with difficult people can empower you to move from grief to greatness.

People did not understand why the Wright Brothers were trying to build a plan to fly. "If God meant for us to fly, he would have given us wings." It is better to let people who do not understand pet loss to stay in the dark than to try to keep on helping them to see the light. The blight of their beliefs may not be right, but your might can keep you in the right. As a result, you can move toward excellence in your life.

Sometimes one needs to stand up and fight for the truth even if others think you are uncouth. It takes integrity to stand firm to do what is right. Sometimes you understand things about yourself that others don't or won't. At other times, other people understand things about you that you don't or want. Life is a balance of making the final choice by giving others a voice. Setting boundaries will prevent other voices from allowing you to make your final choices.

What reality do you need to reconsider? Are you so defensive that others find you offensive? Learning from others leads to excellence. Admitting you are wrong can make you strong. Going on your passionate creative path may lead to others' wrath. Going down your unique path can lead you to refine your life's artistic craft. Life is a balance. Becoming appropriately proactive and being on the offensive can help you reach the goal in the game of life.

We have to make the final decision. Being too directed by others is bad. Being too defensive and self-directed can lead down a needless, bumpy road. Getting off balance with the two can lead to pestilence. Balance can lead you to excellence. Not being able to admit you are wrong and others are right is damaging when it is a pattern. Not being able to stand firm to what you have wisely concluded is like putting out the lantern.

The Serenity Prayer raises these issues regarding relating to difficult people. One needs to know what to strive to change, how to change what one should change, what not to attempt to change, and what is unchangeable. Growing in understanding these tasks as they relate to dealing with thorny people takes serenity, wisdom, and courage.

We can deal with difficult people and stay centered if we have been properly mentored. A sly person is often over-controlling. In some disheartening manner, they may strive to knock one off balance to gain control. In this manner, they can derail another person's feeling of empowerment.

A controlling person wants to be the top dog. Winning by intimidation or some intrusive, uncomfortable method may be their style. Changing what one can and accepting what one cannot change is at the core of coping with devious people. One cannot change difficult people. One can change one's reaction to them. Having the skill to know whether to respond or how to respond to difficult people can help promote serenity within.

A Difficult Neighbor

Many years ago, I had a neighbor with a high-shrill barking dog. It would bark for hours. After a hard day's work, coming home to the sound of this piercing barking rattled my bones. After weeks of tolerating this relentless barking, I approached the neighbor when she was outside. She said she was tired of the barking as well and would solve the problem. The next day, this chronic barking still sent shrill vibrations through the air.

Several attempts were made to try to solve the problem. I went for outside help. The dog shelter came by, and the owner quickly took the dog inside. Being interviewed by the shelter employee was to no avail. The neighbor's remarks led the dog shelter staff to believe that it was my problem. The neighbor hid the dog inside. Then I called the police. The policeman said, "You have a good story, but her story is better."

Then, a few days later, I called the police and had a neighbor as a witness, as he had problems with this person as well. Not only did the policeman believe the witness, he went outside and caught the lady in the act of trying to hide the dog. He told her she had to get him a collar, which would give him a mild shock when he barked. I thought the problem had been solved, but the lady did not put the collar on the dog. The police said I could take her to court. At best, the court would fine her $100, and then the dog would be left to begin barking again. It did not appear that taking the time out for court would be worth it. In an effort to cope with the dog, I began to sing as the dog barked.

We bark, bark, bark all day long.
This barking keeps our lungs strong.
The sound of the barking rises in the air
As an expression to God of two souls in prayer.

I made about twenty rhyming verses, of which the above lines comprised the chorus. It was my way to have some fun regarding a situation in which I had no control. The lady later talked over the fence and said that the prayer had touched her. Her behavior did not really change. My attitude changed by not taking the situation so seriously.

To have a sense of control, we need to feel a sense of centeredness, which results in a feeling of being balanced. An athlete takes an athletic stance to create as much power in his sport as possible. The opposition will strive to get the athlete off-balance. Dealing with difficult people can result in becoming imbalanced.

We can lose our athletic mental stance and consequently lose our effectiveness. We may wish that we did not have to come in contact with obnoxious people. In reality, people have been striving to make other people miserable for thousands of years. As we expand our lives' horizons, we increase the risk of rubbing shoulders with people who may rub us the wrong way.

Difficult people can dilute our effectiveness in the workplace and in every aspect of life. Our reactions to people who are troublesome can be the pivotal point.

We can allow them to diminish us as people or we can become demonstrably larger in dealing with this pervasive challenge. We need to respond in such a fashion that will prevent difficult people from sapping our energies. Our athletic mental agility needs to be kept. Staying centered is needed to hit the bull's eye regarding dealing effectively with people who bully. Then, we can succeed in this challenging arena of life.

Water does run off the backs of ducks. The Serenity Prayer can back us up and give us the backbone to influence difficult people to back down. Our backs will not be against the Wailing Wall. We will not have to buckle under the unnecessary load and stall. The difficult person's behavior will not become debilitating. As we duck we will not become stuck, and we can find experiences that are facilitating.

When I was in the sixth grade, I went out for football. I weighed 100 pounds. It was a very small school in a very small town. The popular guys were the ones who played football. I wanted to be a part of this group. We were taught how to tackle in the initial stages of practice. One by one we were to tackle a person coming directly toward us. We were to demonstrate. The fundamentals of tackling were to be demonstrated.

It came my turn to tackle. The person who was coming toward me was an eighth grader who was solid muscle and weighing 150 pounds. He was eventually on our state championship team during my junior and senior years in high school. As we collided, I tackled him with the correct fundamentals. Then he got up and I did not.

Tackling this person completely knocked the breath out of me, as his knee powered into my stomach. I could barely breathe. The coach came over and loosened my belt. He pulled me up and down by the waist until I began to breath more normally again. We may feel like we have had the breath knocked out of us emotionally if we do not have the coping skills to deal with a difficult person.

Difficult people may be miserable inside. They often deal with their misery by casting their gallstones and kidney stones on those by their side. When someone is a pain, we can use this opportunity as growing pains. A bottle of hot sauce states that, "It hurts so good." Dealing with difficult people can hurt so good and become a spice of life instead of being a slice off our well-being. I began to have fun as every night I would sing with the barking dog.

Dealing with Difficult People: Understanding the Enemy

Coping with the challenging behavior of another depends upon our understanding of ourselves as well as of the other. When we become more insightful about whom we are, we are better prepared to develop skills to counter the culprit. When the culprit is ourselves, we may be more of the problem than the person we are encountering. At a minimum, we will be less skillful in handling the problem. Two difficult people dealing with each other may result in an escalating, reactive, and toxic encounter. The poisonous effects will have no antidote as each person strives to put venom in the cup of the other person's life.

To begin to deal with difficult people, then, we must start with ourselves. We need to become our own best friend. We might take this vow: "I take myself to be my own best friend, to love and to cherish for the rest of my life." A healthy dose of self-esteem can relieve the difficulty we have with ourselves.

When we are hard on ourselves, we can have more difficulty in dealing with people who are hard on us. Then we may not have the foundation to demand respect from others who are not after our own well-being. Having self esteem give us wisdom not to be reactive, but to decide how best to keep the difficult persons behavior on a level field. Then we can cope and not yield.

A difficult person may know our vulnerabilities. With this insight, a devious person can become a detriment to our self-esteem. We may be susceptible to surrendering our power. As a result, we may take a victim's stance. We may feel like prisoners as we feel emotionally captured and controlled by the bully. The reprehensible, offensive behavior may result in our feeling like we are held in captivity.

To offset the person of reproach, we can create within us a sturdy fortress preventing the stones from hitting our heart. People will not likely continue to become difficult to someone that has a high level of self-esteem. When they try to push a person's buttons and it has no power. The difficult person will soon stop as they cannot get on top.

Having painful, underlying feelings can also create a challenge in dealing with difficult people. We may magnify the slightest provocation. As a result, an overreaction resulting from our triggered torment could create an avalanche. Our inner pain can create unwise, reactionary jaunts in overreacting to a difficult person's intentional, revolting taunts. A high self-esteem can provide the basis to allow slights to run off our backs. These putdowns will not feel like heart-stinging smacks. We can healthily detach.

When a difficult person tries to knock us off balance by creating within us a painful, emotional response, we can stay in balance by keeping our self-esteem intact. We can have the foundation to exhibit behaviors that will enable us to stay on course in the midst of encountering a stormy person whose emotions are a negative force. Then we can know that understanding ourselves and becoming our own best friend matters. We can take the bull out of the bully and take what they say as a bunch of bull. Our emotions will be in balance and we can have healthy self-reliance.

Not only do we need to understand ourselves, but we also need to know what makes a difficult person tick. This understanding can prevent them from being like a sucking tick depleting our blood. Difficult people often wear a chip on their shoulders. As a result, they often chip away at the happiness of others. They are hanging on to the past. They feel victimized. Having a lack of empowerment, they resort to manipulation and provocation to gain what they want. Because they have been tormented by someone in the past, they bedevil others in the present.

They have not come to terms with their personal history. Throwing others off balance helps them to feel more stability. Being difficult is not the result of having a bad day. It is their response to having a bad life. Other difficult people may feel entitled because of a background where they have no one to give them a sense of responsibility and accountability.

They have been used to being given things without exerting a sense of effort. Thus, some people become cantankerous because they are greedy. This self-indulgence can result in behaviors that can feel like a cankerous sore to others. It can surface rancor, which they intentionally manifest. We do not have to drink the poison and experience distress.

Dealing with Difficult People Can Be Unnerving.
They Can Cause the Car of Our Lives to Begin Swerving.

—Dan Crenshaw

Possessions may be more important to other people. To get what they want, they may use other people. They are not team players. The rules of fair play are not utilized. Their aggressive behavior is insensitive to the consequences they create in the lives of people they encounter. They are only interested in how others can be used to meet their own self-centered needs.

Some people are difficult because they have a substance abuse problem or mental illness or both. These people can become very difficult to deal with because they may be in denial. We do not need to take other people's problems as our own or we will gradually feel a sharp pain that will cut to the bone.

Some people may become temporarily difficult because they are sick or tired. This is not pervasive behavior. They are having a bad day as a result of being temporarily stressed out. Their minds, bodies, and spirits are momentarily overloaded.

In extreme cases, people are malicious, evil, and dangerous. They are frighteningly destructive in their behavior. Encountering a person of this nature may require police protection. They need external controls such as a jail to keep them in check. There are no inner reins and they have to be reined in.

Understanding difficult people can help us maintain some objectivity and rational thought. Then we are able to keep proper emotional distance by not taking the difficult people's reactions personally. You may realize that the behavior is a pervasive problem in the person's life. Others have been the brunt of the person's scheming actions. Difficult people can often be understood. This understanding can keep us out of the woods. We will not take their actions and words personally. We can be wise and deal with them skillfully.

Focused confrontation can diffuse difficult people. I remember that when I as a pastor, I gathered people around me who consented to being on a steering committee to work to organize a volunteer chaplaincy program in a hospital. These volunteers were to minister to people who had no pastor or who were in a crisis situations. Another role involved being a liaison to the pastor of a person in the hospital.

During the first meeting to begin organizing the volunteer group, one of the ministers said, "You will never get busy ministers to join you in this venture." I then responded by saying," You consented to being on this committee. Why have you decided not to support its mission?" From that time forward, he did not stand in the way of the effort, which became a resounding success.

Dealing with difficult people can be a positive stroke. When I was a student at a seminary, I substitute taught in the inner city schools in a very difficult time. On one occasion, I turned around from writing on the blackboard to find the students in a circle with two students face to face with each other ready to fight. The other students had picked up their desks and formed a circle around the students.

I went up to them and one student said, "Teacher, take your glasses off. I am going to beat your head in." I told him that I bet he could beat me up if he wanted to. He said, "Yes, I could." Then he went back to his seat and sat down. A stroke to his ego had stabilized a difficult situation. It was a positive leverage that brought calmness to the classroom setting. He no longer had any reason to prove anything to his peers. Of course, this way of dealing with this particular situation may not work with all people. It may take another approach.

Here are some other examples of what to say in more normal circumstances when people are angry. "Here are your options," or "Have you tried . . ." or "Let's talk about this for a minute." An angry person wants to be heard and respected. Listen to an angry person. Listening can calm a difficult person's anger. Give the person the opportunity to vent their rancor. Don't trivialize it, but don't over-validate it either.

I can see that you're angry. Is there anything else you would like to say?" Recognizing their anger, giving them respect may reduce their anger's intensity. Reason in communication may prevail, and one may open up an opportunity to problem solve. Developing a repertoire of behaviors can be the leverage to equalize the power. By giving them respect and not power struggling, agreeing to disagree may become an option. We can gain the foundation to develop behaviors to best respond to people who have the motivation to rob us of our good day.

Forgiveness: A Wise Choice in Responding to Thorny People

A difficult person's behavior can sometimes leave a gash. This infected wound will not quickly dash. Forgiveness can feel insurmountable to begin, but it can be a process if healing within. Effectively dealing with difficult people may require a forgiving spirit. Letting go of one's bitterness and feeling of wanting revenge may be the most difficult task of all.

If someone shot and killed your loved one, you would not say immediately, "I forgive you. You must have had a bad day." This is similar to the grief process. One has to go through stages in order to come to terms with the damage of the underserved trauma. Otherwise it would be premature forgiveness. One must allow oneself to feel the impact of the injustice and work through the hurt and anger. One can begin the journey of healing and prevent the impact of the event from eating one alive. Forgiveness is not for the fainthearted, but it may help keep one from fainting.

To forgive another person should not be a simple matter. It is a process of working through a mixture of feelings that sits on one's platter. If one partakes of the platter, it can eat one alive. Your life can then take a nose dive. You can gradually reduce what is on your plate. This reduction can begin to ease the almost unbearable heartache. Forgiveness has to come when it is time. The time is never perfect. At some point, one needs to make the decision to forgive and begin to come to terms with the injustice that they did not deserve.

It is not always wise to attempt to communicate directly with the other person. A face-to-face connection could make the wound worsen. One forgives to heal one's own anger. It can be done between oneself and God to diminish the rancor. One may not completely recover from such a trauma. Complete forgiveness may not be obtained, but if one can go halfway up the mountain, at least some of the vistas can bring relief from a trauma to the soul. One can begin to let go of the bitterness and pain.

The person that has been wrenched by an unmerciful trauma can find rest in granting pardon. A quenched soul at rest can be fertile ground resulting from a forgiving heart. Forgiveness can bring back the flavor to one's life. The enormity of the difficulty of forgiveness can be overcome. The fruits of one's labor can be harvested. As one begins the harvesting process, it is important that one realizes that forgiveness gets one off the hook but not the perpetrator. What this person does in the sanctuary of their souls is their responsibility.

None of us are professional forgivers. We need to take the leap and start the process toward getting feelings behind us. Sunlight can break through a cloud of cynicism. The chip on a difficult person's shoulder will no longer chip away at our fulfillment in life. In grief, we may have to forgive. In life, we will have to forgive.

We will then know that forgiveness matters, and we can gain a sense of control. Our lives will not be imprisoned by festering resentment. We will no longer be preoccupied about the past. We will be occupied in changing what we can. Learning the art of dealing with this thorny challenge well can keep our thoughts on difficult people from wanting to dwell.

Good Boundaries Are Necessary for Healthy Relational Coping Skills.

Healthy boundaries keep one in the game of life. Knowing who to let in and how close can prevent much strife. Boundaries can be harmful or beneficial. Destructive boundaries can leave us wandering in the desert. Effective boundaries can help us reach the promise land.

One can build a boundary with a wall ten feet high.

It will certainly keep a person safe and no one will be nigh. Also, one will be very lonely and bored, and they may wish that they had more treasured memories stored. One may be wise to put on the wall a gate. Then one can put more memories on their plate. One can open and close the gate to prevent indigestion. Then one will be safer and healthier without question.

When an infant is born, the baby has no sense of boundaries. The infant feels that it merges into its environment. A newborn infant has no sense of its individual self. The infant is a part of the universe, and the universe is a part of the infant. At the age of two, the child works to begin gaining a sense of autonomy by using the word *no.*

Thus, the terrible twos begin. This stage becomes difficult for parents. It is important for the child to learn to say no. *No* is a formidable word that is absolutely necessary to protect one's boundaries. While many two-year-old children overuse the word, they need to learn the word in order to gradually gain a balance between yes and no as they mature.

It would be nice if the child would comply with every wish of the parent. Without the word *no*, we would be defenseless in the midst of the demands of life. We would have no boundaries. There would be no spaces in our togetherness.

Good Boundaries: Bound for the Promise Land
Good boundaries are necessary for us to pursue
purpose, passion, and excellence.
As they can keep you from going through undue pestilence.

—Dan Crenshaw

Healthy boundaries keep one in the game of life. Knowing who to let in and how close can prevent much strife. Boundaries can give us a healthy sense of control to keep conniving people's behavior from taking its toll. Just as the ocean waves coming ashore can erode the beauty of the beach, lacking boundaries can cause erosion in our emotional and spiritual health.

Millions of dollars are spent each year to help beaches recover from the devastating impact of erosion. Billions of dollars are spent in helping people recover from stress-related illnesses resulting from weak boundaries. These illnesses result from not taking care of themselves and letting the "wolf huff and puff and blow the house down."

Boundaries are preventative tools. They are crucial in creating a buffer to protect us from others who want to rule. It can prevent them from being cruel. It can take away their destructive fuel. We need to draw a line in the sand to prevent us from succumbing to a person's unreasonable demand.

When a fly or a mosquito violates our boundaries, we become agitated and do all we can to eradicate the intruder. An insect repellent keeps them at bay. Then we can relax at the bay. A healthy sense of self-esteem can be the foundation of building a boundary to keep others from violating our boundaries.

We are in control. This foundation can prevent us from floundering by being wisely bold. We are the executive of our lives. The decisions that we make can allow a balance between saying yes and saying no. We can prevent ourselves from being a fodder, eating up by the hungry, ravenous, selfish appetites of others.

Unhealthy Boundaries: Who Is Most Susceptible?

> *When boundaries have been broken when one was a child,*
> *One's behavior can violate others as one becomes wild.*
> *An opposite reaction is not using boundaries as protection.*
> *The person may open their door at the slightest suggestion.*

> *—Dan Crenshaw*

People who have severe problems with boundaries often have been struck with repeated blows emotionally and physically. Their boundaries may have been violated with verbal, physical, or sexual abuse. They may be left broken emotionally.

Boundaries can prevent one from being misused and can ward off being abused. One can gradually heal until the damage is diminished. Then one's healing has almost finished. Having no boundaries may strike a chord within us to be free. It is exciting to see films of horses in the Wild West running free. We are not created to run wild.

On the other hand, we do not need to be corralled like wild horses and put in a fence. Good fences may make good neighbors, but the fences need to have a gate in order for us to be neighborly. Otherwise we will say "Nay, nay, nay" like the corralled horse.

Boundaries need flexible gates to allow a trusting person to give us a helping hand. Then we can become empowered to change what we can. Having a low self-esteem resulting from boundary violations may leave a person with challenges. They may try to be accepted by others by pleasing others without regard to their own needs. They may allow themselves to be used or manipulated by others. They have lost the ability to say no sufficiently to provide balance.

The Dead Sea does not support life because it has no outlet. The water evaporates and leaves a growing residue of salt. A life that has no outlet can become emotionally dead. Saying no allows one to fill the river of their lives. Saying yes provides an outlet of service or a way to contribute to other's lives.

On the other hand, people with low self-esteem may try to feel better by acting out their pain, bullying others, or violating others' needs. They look for vulnerable targets that may be people who act in their pain. People with low self-worth may deprecate themselves and focus primarily on others.

This is fulfilling to them, as it helps them to avoid focusing on their own inner pain. It is often said that one way to feel better is to help someone else. This is certainly true to a point. Taken to the extreme, it can burn a person out because their own cup can run on empty in the process.

With care and persistence, people can recover from control malfunctions. They can, through the help of others, reconstruct their lifestyle and produce the beautiful person that God intends for them to be. They can look back at their traumas and find the broken child in them emerging from the hammer blows to become beautifully sculptured. They can fashion a life that becomes a fashion statement. This fashion statement emphatically declares that they have a right to honor their limits and move toward their possibilities. Healthy boundaries do matter.

Boundaries: A Balancing Act

> *Balancing yes and no prevents too much from being on one's plate.*
> *This balance prevents one from developing a chronic emotional ache*
>
> —Dan Crenshaw

Gaining a sense of healthy boundaries is truly a balancing act. As a child, I remember wanting to play on a seesaw during recess. I found a friend much larger than myself and began to try to seesaw. It was very difficult, if not impossible, because the seesaw was weighted down on my friend's side. There was not a nice up-and-down flow. The weight distribution was not equal, and it became very tiring.

Life is a marathon, not a mad dash. We will not finish the race carrying someone continuously on our backs. It needs to be noted that sometimes there are no easy answers. A person with a handicapped child has a particularly tough challenge in setting boundaries. The task can at times become overwhelming, and gaining proper help may not be readily forthcoming.

If we choose to keep our lives out of balance, we may find ourselves overreacting to situations with anger. It is certainly different when we are dealing with a crisis or a trauma. This is a temporary situation that can try one's soul. A lifestyle of overextending ourselves can leave us in the desert lost and not being able to find life-giving water. The seesaw in the flow of life is not balanced. Life is not working well and is not fulfilling.

Oftentimes, the oldest child chooses a lifestyle that becomes overly responsible. Many executives are the oldest child. Some of the strongest leaders are older children. But many burn out because they do not set boundaries. They will be working when they need to be soaking up love and having enriching experiences that feed their soul.

Self-esteem means that one gives but also takes care of oneself.
They do not always have to continually make
gifts like Santa Claus' little elves.

Self-esteem is not arrogance. Healthy self-esteem helps one to balance life and not become sucked dry by life's demands. In a balanced seesaw experience, the push of one person gives the other person a nice ride. Then, the initial pusher receives a nice ride as the other person pushes down. These boundaries help life to flow, and we will not buckle under the heavy weight of another person.

Self-esteem helps one's life not to become lost in the shuffle. One will know when their feathers are beginning to ruffle.

Boundaries: Not the Same for Everyone

Healthy boundaries for each person can be unique.
Some people need more space to function at their peak.

—Dan Crenshaw

There is no cookie-cutter production line for all to follow. We have individual differences. Healthy boundaries in one person may be different from that of another person. For example, a dog's boundaries are very different from a cat's. A dog will immediately respond when its master calls. A cat may say, "I will be in touch with you later."

At times, cats seem to be aloof to their own world. Dogs are more extroverted, and they need much more attention from their master. Often they need much more exercise. They need less time for themselves than a cat, and each style works. If it is not broken, do not fix it. In comparison to someone else, your boundaries may seem unhealthy. Appearances may be deceiving as you have a different mental and emotional makeup.

Consequently, just as cats and dogs have differences in boundaries, humans have differences as well. The range of healthy differences may not be as wide as dogs' and cats', but extroverts are going to be more like dogs. They need less boundaries for alone time. Introverts are like cats in that they can be contented spending more time by themselves.

Thus, extroverts often marry introverts. They seem to complement each other. One can be the center of attention, and the other can feel comfortable being in the background. The extrovert can be a good talker, and the introvert can be a good listener. The extrovert may be intense, and the introvert may be calm. These complimentary traits can have a tranquilizing effect for the extrovert and can energize the introvert.

Later in the relationship these qualities that initially attracted the couple to each other can begin to create conflict. The extrovert may wonder why the introvert wants to leave the party so early. They may fight like cats and dogs. Couples then must be sensitive to each other's differences so they will be able to handle conflicts less reactively.

Each person has different needs in being alone.
Needs must be honored or conflict can cut to the bone.
One partner to gain distance may push the other away.
That is the only way they feel they can keep them at bay.

—*Dan Crenshaw*

Perhaps that is why some dogs do not like cats. The boundaries are at two ends of the spectrum. On the other hand, couples can like each other. They can compromise and enjoy the complementary aspects of their personalities. The relationship can be viable as both vie for a successful connection.

Boundaries: They Give Us Our Identity

Healthy boundaries define who we are.
We say yes and no to keep ourselves from becoming ajar.

—Dan Crenshaw

Some people have weak boundaries. Their lives may become out of control as they have little control over people infringing upon their rights. They are then very susceptible to a person who may strive to control their lives for the controlling person's benefit.

If you look at a map of the United States, each state is easily distinguishable by boundaries. Each state has a unique shape. As people, we gain our identity by the boundaries that we set. We know when we end and when other people begin. Two questions are raised in our identity: "Who am I?" and "Who am I not?" Boundaries tell us what state the body of land is and what territory is not a part of the state.

I was born as an identical twin. My brother and I dressed just alike, and many people called us twin. They could not tell us apart. It was cute for us to be together, but it hindered gaining a sense of identity. Gradually we emerged as two separate people with unique strengths and weaknesses.

If boundaries in the United States were too rigid, people would not be able to travel around the country and learn the uniqueness of each state. In the same light, when people have rigid boundaries, people around them will not get to know them.

Boundaries need to be permeable. Osmosis must take place as contact is made. Emotions and ideas need to seep back and forth to have a true engagement. Boundaries that are too rigid will be like the turtle that will not stick its head out of the shell. The inner life is hidden by a fortress, which blocks the entry of other people into its unique state of mind.

On the other hand, if the turtle lost its shell and had no boundaries, it would not be recognizable. It would also be defenseless against predators. It would lose its identity and its life. Boundaries, then, can give us identity as well as a balanced life.

The United States would become chaotic if the states lost their boundaries. States would lose their identity if they merged into each other and we did not know where one began and ended. It would not be recognizable, and its unique identity would die. States then need boundaries for identity, but they also need permeability for connection with other states and the federal government. States could not be all that they could be without this connection. We could not become all we would be without linkages.

Boundaries give identity, and we grow by having a welcome sign that invites others into our world. Each state and most towns have a welcome sign as an invitation to enter their unique world, and the states are better off for it. No person needs to be like an island. They will feel like a castaway in a faraway land. Having a welcome mat signals to others they can get to know us. They know that inquiring about our lives will not create a fuss.

The following questions will always be raised: How autonomous should the states be to remain at their optimal health? How dependent should they be upon the federal government? In a friendship or marriage, how much space and autonomy should there need to be? How much connection and independence should there be for optimal health?

The turf or boundaries of workers in the workplace gives definition to the job. There is a job description. If the turf or boundaries are too rigid, it will keep teamwork from creating synergy. Ideas flowing from the top to the bottom as well as from the bottom to the top create optimal health for the company.

Boundaries: Not Too Rigid or Too Weak

We are created for uniqueness, and we are created for relationships. This uniqueness goes for naught if boundaries are too rigid. Uniqueness is lost if boundaries are too weak. We need boundaries to know who we are. We need connection with others to maximize our potential. Then we can experience that healthy boundaries matter.

A friend once said the greatest challenges of middle age is coming to terms to those who have hurt us, to those people we have hurt, and coming to terms to ways we have hurt ourselves. Forgiveness can give us freedom to let go and seize opportunities of life when they come our way.

In many research projects, it has been proven over and over again that sour relationships can be more than a successful job can possibly stand. Relationships can become so noxious that the company and the relationships will disband. As a result, one may find that an ability to skillfully relate holds in its hands one's employment fate. Good relationships can enable one to cope with challenges on the job. Then one will not have to fail and ultimately sob.

Marriage Relationship: The Most Challenging Relationship of All

Relationships can be a balm of comfort that increases coping skills or bombs of explosions that can greatly cripple our ability to deal with life. The most complex relationship is the marriage relationship. These principles can enhance any relationship. Then relationships can increase one's ability to cope and enable one to move toward purpose, passion, and excellence.

Taming control/change issues in marriage is the centerpiece of a good relationship. Trying to change one's marriage partner in the wrong manner will not grant one a welcome home banner. The banner will surely come down tattered and torn, canceling the welcoming home banner and leaving both spouses forlorn.

One highway sign alerts us that we need to merge into flowing traffic. As we merge, we need to have spaces in our togetherness to prevent a wreck. Relationships can ultimately collide if there is too little distance in their togetherness. Also, a relationship can become derailed if there is too much distance for true intimacy.

The partners need to bond and feel very near to each other.
If they are too close and have no distance, they may become a bother.

In terms of control, boundaries give balance to relational control. "Lord, help us to change what we can." To implement that prayerful request in a constructive manner, we need to understand boundaries. If we are people who are over-controlling, we become intrusive and unwelcome guests in other people's space in an attempt to change them.

One who has allowed someone to violate one's space may feel that one is being held hostage and has no breathing room. They may freeze and set themselves up to become victims. The deer-in-the-headlight look does not fare well.

One may not get out of the way of oncoming traffic. As a result, one may become injured by the person who has intruded one's space. Consequently, if one indiscriminately lets others in one's space and does not get out of one's way, ones may feel like one's life is a wreck.

As we balance life, we need space,
And boundaries give us our needed private place.

Knowing what to change and how to change what one can change can prevent us from sticking our noses into the wrong places. For example, intruding upon the responsibilities of others and taking them on as our own can overwhelm our minds, bodies, and spirits, making us a pawn. One may begin to slowly sink in the quicksand and become the victim.

This tragic dynamic commonly happens with the spouse of a person who is addicted to alcohol. The relationship does not have proper rhythm as one continues to drop the ball. The other keeps picking up the ball, and the relationship begins to stall.

The spouse often enables the behavior of the person with an alcohol problem. For example, they may strive to cushion the blow of the repercussions of their spouse's drinking. The spouse rescues the problem drinker from the consequences of their behavior, enabling their destructive behavior to continue.

This enabling behavior inhibits their spouse's impetus to reach out for help. The enabler becomes a chronic safety net. This net prevents the person with alcoholism from hitting bottom and bouncing back up into a new way of life.

The price of sticking one's nose in the business of the person with an alcohol problem can indeed erode the sanity of the enabler. Their needs are getting lost. An enabler can increase their fervor, placing their lives on a feverously unhealthy path. This self-destructive path of both partners can in up with the enabler ultimately experiencing wrath.

Well-meaning, Overzealous Fervor Can Backfire on the Server.

Changing this pattern can be a win-win for both the person with alcoholism and the spouse. The person with alcoholism can find their true selves and begin a path of growth. The spouse can be freed from the entanglement of enabling behavior. There is also the danger that the person with the alcohol problem will not, at least at this time, change. But they now know that the ball is in their court. They will begin to have to look at themselves in the mirror and see the overlooked wart.

Then the enabling spouse will learn when the ball is in their court with responsibility, and when the ball is in the spouse's court with irresponsibility. As a result, boundaries can be like floodgates, keeping the unrealistic demands of the person with alcoholism from drowning the spouse. Then the right amount of water can douse the fire and prevent it from burning down the house.

Over-controlling Can Wreck Relationships

We need to have a listening ear to keep over-controlling in the rear. Nothing flies in the face of intimacy and relationships more than control issues. When aspects of control become out of control, they can become a menace to a marriage. Misusing power in an effort to change one's mate can mangle a relationship. As a result, both mates can become entangled.

In the game of chess, the match ends when one player corners the other and gains the position of checkmate. The other player then has no move left. In a spousal relationship, if only one mate wins, the whole relationship loses. Consequently, in the game of life, the move of checkmate may become "wreck mate." The couple will not be a good match. The relationship may end in the game of life. One partner is controlled and cornered. There is no move left.

Control can cause a relationship to sail or rail. Control can cause a relationship to be sound or to drown. Often when couples come together striving to control each other, communication can become highly conflicted. It may feel like they are two porcupines with their quills sticking out. These quills can torment each other.

If one partner has quills and the other partner has feathers, the feathers may be ruffled. It behooves both partners to transform their quills into feathers. Then, as they deal with control issues, they can discuss issues with less dissension. Communication will have a softer, less intense tone. The conversation will be more collaborative and promote positive change. Each partner will have an additional "feather in their cap."

Control matters can bring focus or fret. Issues out of control can cause a relationship to soar or sour. The manner in which one strives to create change can instill beauty or become beastly. Communication can create a Jekyll or a Hyde. Communication can promote frankincense or Frankenstein.

Too much stress can be the culprit that promotes the porcupine's approach to dealing with differences. This approach creates a bristling "attack and react" pattern which sets the stage for walls instead of bridges.

A selfish use of power creates painful barriers and dangerous, deep ridges. If a spouse breaks down the wall, they may then trip and fall.

When stress is managed well, it sets the stage for getting the train back on the track. The climate is conducive for dialogue. Couples can learn to enjoy coupling and intimacy. Consequently, they will know that getting control issues under control matters. Uncontrollable issues can fuel the fires of hate. Harnessing control can benefit one's mate. The outcome of the marriage then may exude a good fate.

In striving to change what should be changed, bonding and intimacy require that a couple take the reins together in charting the course of their relationship. Both partners need to feel that they have an influence. They both need to feel that they have a voice that is heard and heeded.

When partners do not over-control, they allow each other's differences to unfold. Each partner has their own uniqueness to give to the mix.

They do not see each one's differences as something to fix. Control issues go awry when the integrity of one partner is compromised by the demands of the other. Love involves demonstrating concern regarding their partner's growth and well-being.

The following are two conversations that represent positive and negative communication.

> *When communication becomes nonnegotiable demands*
> *The relationship can become severed with relentless commands.*
> *The relationships may begin profusely bleeding.*
> *If each partner does not begin heeding,*
> *Their relation will not begin succeeding.*

> —Dan Crenshaw

Spouse 1: "Honey, I am quitting work and going to school to become a lawyer."

Spouse 2: "We have not even discussed the matter."

Spouse 1: "What is there to discuss? The decision has already been made."

Spouse 2: "I will be the one carrying the kids to their activities, and I will spend three times as much time taking care of them."

Spouse 1: "You will learn what I have been going through."

When communication exudes deep-abiding respect,
A mate may be prevented from wanting to hit the deck.
Resolution can occur when each partner feels respected and safe.
Then a win-win can result in the mates wanting to mate.

—Dan Crenshaw

The following interchange is an alternative and kinder, gentler approach, which can avert agonizing reproach.

Spouse 1: "I am seriously thinking about going back to school and becoming a lawyer."
Spouse 2: "I am so proud of your ambition. I think you will be very successful. We do need to discuss how we are going to divide responsibilities with the children and household chores.
Spouse 1: "I know that this is going to place more responsibility on you. I will have to cut back some. We can discuss how we will adjust and come up with some agreeable plan."
Spouse 2: "You helped put me through school, and you deserve the same."
Spouse 1: "Thank you for caring about a very important aspect of my life."

Control can become orders or develop into a change agent, influencing harmonious order. When control issues are out of control, one partner's growth is stunted. The spouse who is over-controlling may treat their mate as if they are simply extensions of their own needs. Then, the needs of the partner are compromised.

They do not feel that their partner is out for their best interest. The couple is not taking care of each other. As a result, they are full of care, burdened by having to cope with the dysfunctional relationship. Despondency and eroding hope diminish the present meaning of marriage. A better understanding of control issues can be brought to light by comparing three different kinds of relationships.

One relationship is like two circles that are side by side and do not intersect. There is no real bond. They are more like roommates. In their comings and goings, their lives do not intersect. They may engage in conversation as if they were passing on the street.

Communication is limited to the needs of living in the same house. Bonding needs are not met. Couples who are not getting along place activities in between the relationship to keep distance. One can spend more time at work, golfing, having separate activities, etc. The affairs of one's life can serve as damaging affairs to the marriage.

Some couples are like two ships passing in the night.
Their beating hearts are out of sound and sight.

—Dan Crenshaw

With unresolved issues looming, closeness is uncomfortable. Consequently, their lives may move further and further apart until there is no genuine bond. Some couples live like this for years. Other couples may terminate the marriage. Some couples are able to improve communication and move toward bonding.

Next, there is the circle that intersects. This intersection represents a nice bond with each person's individuality honored. The couple feels that their individual, separate lives are growing while their relationship is strengthening.

Some couples are like two ships that are passing in the day.
Their hearts are in sight and sound as they stop together and stay.
For a while they part, and they take a piece of
the treasure of their partner's heart.
The bond is still there, even though the two ships have parted for a while.
They later return to the dock and give each other a warm, welcoming smile.

—Dan Crenshaw

Sharing mutually enjoyable activities can help strengthen bonding. An example of a relaxing, engaging time is hiking. In hiking, communing with the beauty of nature can bring down walls and helps one to commune with each other verbally and nonverbally. Walls come down, as the stressful distractions dissipate into the background.

The beauty of nature's masterful artwork absorbs all attention and plunges one in the present moment where all that came before and all that will come after is nonexistent. The present is all that matters, and the foundation for nurturing a relationship is built. Intimacy and closeness are the priceless results. Romance can be expressed by words, but the experience goes beyond words. When no word needs to be said, romance is in its deepest state. A deep connection is mutually felt.

Finally, there is the circle within a circle that depicts one partner overpowering the other. These two circles illustrate when control issues are out of control. The relationship is a one-way street. Traffic is going in only one direction. If one partner strives to go down the one-way street believing it is a two-way road, the partners will collide. One spouse is reading a one-way sign and the other spouse is reading a two-way sign. One person will be dying inside, and the relationship can become a total wreck.

A caricature of the over-controlling relationship may also be graphically depicted by a Balboa snake coiled around its prey. Many people in a controlling relationship say that they are feeling smothered because they do not feel safe to be themselves. The partner who is controlling often lives with pain inside. They act out their pain, and the spouse may act in their anguish. To promote peace, the latter spouse may placate.

Unbridled control creates an unhappy spouse.
The controlled mate may then experience the partner as a louse.

Many marriages end up in a crisis if the controlled partner calls for the other partner's hand. They are tired of their partner playing with a stacked deck when they are living with a deck of cards that are stacked against them. Under the intimidation, one spouse may want to "hit the deck." There is a danger that the marriage may dissolve, but there is also an opportunity for true intimacy to take place, creating mutual harmony.

Control can cause a relationship to flounder or create a tasty flounder.
Control can cause the marriage to be a famine or a feast.

The apple cart has been turned upside down. The stage has been set. The partners can pick up the apples and start throwing them at each other. An escalating, conflictive communication pattern may ensue. On the other hand, the partners have the opportunity to put the apples back in the cart in a manner that can enliven their marriage.

There is then the possibility for the marriage to be a two-way street. The traffic can flow in both directions. Both voices can be heard. The couple then feels that they are influencing each other. As a result, they feel that their relationship is being mutually fed. They will feel that they both exhibit good manners.

When differences occur, the partner can strive for a win-win. This form of communication can help deeper intimacy to begin.

One person does not talk and only hear the echo of their own voice. They really listen and heed the unique voice and preferential choice of their partner. This person does not see the other as an extension of his needs. They are now looking for a person who has their own unique voice, and they are giving that voice permission to be heard.

They are not simply enamored by the sound of their voice. They are willing for their partner to make their unique choice.

They realize that listening and respecting the distinctive voice of the partner is vital. In communication, one must not catch an idea that the partner has thrown to them, drop it, and then pick up another ball and throw it back. This behavior becomes a way to divert attention away from the issue that has been brought to the table.

The crisis can be dangerous if the spouse's different voice is not heard. The calamity of control can be avoided as the partner listens to every word. The relationship may be bruised, as the spouse's request for the partner to listen is refused. Then the relationship can feel like it is being refused. To be discarded at the city dump for no use. Then the relationship may end up feeling like trash. It can overheat and become like a mountain of ash.

Ponder this conversation between the partners of this couple:

In the first dialogue, one spouse's voice was not heard or heeded.
In the second, both voices were heard, making each one feel needed.

Spouse 1: "I need to talk with you regarding how you can help more around the house."

Spouse 2: "Well, I need to talk with you about how you can be more sensitive to how tired I am when I come home from work."

Spouse 1: "That is an interesting response. I have a very demanding job as I work as well. I also do all the housework."

Spouse 2: "You need to think about doing more yard work too."

One partner side-stepping the issue
Can create tears in their mate, resulting in a need for a tissue.

The following spouses are dealing with the issue that is brought to the table,
And they are in step with a successful solution because they are able.

Spouse 1: "I need to talk with you regarding how you can help more around the house."

Spouse 2: "It sounds like having to do all the housework is very difficult."

Spouse 1: "Yes, especially since I have recently received a promotion. I come home and just do not have the energy to do it all."

Spouse 2: "What can I do to help?"

Spouse 1: "It would be a great help if you would wash the dishes after I cook."

Spouse 2: "That sounds fair. Is there anything else I can do?"

Spouse 1: "It is very sensitive of you to ask how you can help. It keeps me from beginning to yelp. Taking out the trash is becoming more difficult for me.

That would be a great aid if you would gather the trash, place it in the bin, and roll it out to the curb." (Saying tongue-in-cheek.) Then, I will not have to kick you to the curb. [Giggle

Spouse 2: "Okay. Let's execute the plan and then see how it goes."

Spouse 1: "That sounds like a plan. I hope I do not get executed." [Giggle]

Responding to the distinctive voice of their partner can create a relationship of distinction. One can feel more relaxed and safe to infuse humor in the relationship as well.

Humor is the positive addiction that gives a couple a natural high.
Wit can create a relationship that says, "My oh my."

Comedy can Help Prevent a Tragedy

A relationship that contains comedy can become a blissful rhapsody. The mate can sign a love letter, "Deliriously yours." Then the fun-filled, healthy, crazy relationship will not feel like a chore.

Silliness and seriousness can shake hands to form a more serene relationship. In the right manner, humor can be the oil to prevent inertia and sparks from relational friction.

The balance between the sublime and the ridiculous can keep the seesaw smoothly going up and down to tickle the stomachs of the relationships.

Silliness can bring serenity, resulting in peaceful, emotional, relational safety. Safety can then instill a sense of security.

Security can culminate in trust, resulting in a strong relational bond. Trusting can prevent a relationship from rusting.

Thus, humor can help one transcend a difficult situation and accept what one cannot change. Laughter then reduces stress and helps one to transcend problems that are not solvable.

Furthermore, humor can help make the solvable problem more amenable to revealing a solution.

Humor then has many amenities. It has many spin-offs that can keep the relationship spinning and the heads and hearts swimming. Coping with thorny issues frees couples to experience a bouquet of laughter and joy.

Silliness and serenity can then prevail over stress and enmity. As a result, healthy, crazy relationships can help a couple to become crazy about each other. A playful relationship can play into the hands of a good-natured marriage. Control issues will be tamed by a sense of lightness that keeps stress from making marriage a mess. Not having interdependence can create power struggles. Reactivity can emerge, and problem-solving can be muddled.

Pursue Distance--Another Way Control Goes Awry.

Pursue-distance pattern of relating can be changed when one does not feel controlled. The pattern needs to be changed before the relationship becomes very old. As this pattern changes, the partner begins to feel more at ease. The spouse may feel like a cure has eradicated a painful disease. Then one may say, "Catch me if you can and you can. You are the man."

Professional surfers say that their lives are at stake as they ride a wave. As they are surfing the gigantic powerful wave, they have to be very skillful. One wrong move can place them in harm's way. Instead of having the thrill of riding the powerful wave, they could be killed as they helplessly experience the brutal churning of the wave's overwhelming might.

This scene depicts many men's fear of intimacy. They fear losing their own autonomy and becoming helplessly engulfed in the power of the relationship. A dominating mother may have stifled their growth. Additionally, they may have experienced their mother dominating their father. Thus, they may set distance as their wife pursues.

As a result, a wife may feel that she has no power to enable a positive outcome to ensue. Her pursuit may escalate and intensify. Then the man may escalate his distancing immensely. The twain shall never meet. When the man distances himself, the woman feels the relationship will never become sweet.

As her attempts to engage her husband are discounted, she may feel that her needs do not matter. Her words may feel like meaningless chatter. She may not be able to influence her husband at all. As a result, she may feel that she is talking to a brick wall. In a relationship, if one partner is always the one to pursue, a relationship that has a widening gap will probably ensue.

Then the pursuing partner may begin the conversations with harsher start-ups. The partner may strive desperately to achieve contact to have some influence on the relationship but only disrupts. The other spouse, feeling vulnerable, may withdraw to avoid a fight. Both have reasons for their behavior, and they feel that they are right. With the continuation of the negative communication pattern, the pursue-distance dynamic may intensify. The crack in the bond may become more difficult to rectify.

Communication may take the form of a blame and withdraw pattern. The fire of passion in the relationship has turned into an ominous cold dark cavern. One partner may feel emotionally battered, while the other may feel very tattered. The relationship may be marred, as both partners feel profoundly scarred.

The pursue-distance dynamic, which may involve a myriad of issues, may intensify as the feelings of being rejected and used become greater. Thus, each partner may take turns going into hibernation and say, "I may see you later." Thus, one partner may turn a cold shoulder to avoid the painful feeling of being controlled. The other spouse may give up in despair, feeling like their increasingly desperate pursuit is resulting in a stronger refute.

Many couples find themselves in this pursue-distance relational pattern. This pattern is a futile way of avoiding being controlled. This cat-and-mouse chase can create a fit of frenzy. When the cat is away, the mouse will play. When the cat comes back, it darkens the mouse's day. The hide-and-seek pattern can sour attempts of contact. If this pursue-distance pattern continues, intimacy in the relationship may be in jeopardy.

The spousal relationship is in danger as this negative relational pattern undermines one partner's influence. Thus, control issues can become out of control as one partner has no mutually gratifying impact on the other. There is no opportunity to negotiate a win-win solution. Mutual giving and receiving is null and void.

A couple may exit from this cycle of exile by communicating in a softer tone. This non-attacking tone can be more engaging. The conversational tone may be akin to the way the couple communicated when they were engaged. When the cat comes back, then the mouse will play. The cat will no longer be catty and drive the mouse batty. The cat will go to bat for the mouse, and the cat will no longer act like a louse.

Quills can turn into feathers, and a dialogue can take place. The twain can meet as they feel comfortable face to face. Mutual contact can contain more grace. There is no longer a cat-and-mouse chase. They have a mutually fulfilling pace. There is no feeling of relational disgrace. The flowers in their relationship are blossoming in their vase. There is now a comfortable relational cohesion instead of a lamentable relational lesion.

Triggers: Learning to Become Trigger-Happy

Triggers are vulnerable spots that stem from the past. They are hurt places inside that continue to last. When a partner pushes this button after becoming mad, it can make the mate deeply sad. Getting control issues under control, then, also involves understanding triggers.

Triggers occur when one partner's behavior or words strike a painful chord in the other's emotional system.

The broken string hurts when it is plucked. Instead of providing music of harmony, it can promote discord. For example, a woman or a man may speak harshly, and the partner may become triggered. Residual, underlying feelings lingering from past verbal abuse as a child may erupt. Too many pushed triggers can create many rigors.

The resulting music is not pleasing to the emotional ears. The painful feelings are reverberations of anguish that one has experienced early in one's life. These painful feelings are echoing and creating disharmony and static in the present. As a result, a partner may overreact to the situation at hand.

For example, many people experience abandonment issues. Abandonment feelings occur in many ways for a child. Underlying painful feelings of fear of being cast aside may occur if the adult was abused by someone they trusted. Feelings of being forsaken may also have originated when the adult was emotionally deprived by distancing, disengaged parents. These underlying feelings of being discarded can play out in a relationship in the form of over-controlling.

One partner may strive to overly control their mate for fear of losing them. Intimidation and fear may be used to strive to keep the partner under control. They may beat down their partner emotionally until the partner feels that they have no separate, autonomous self. The controlling partner may treat their spouse like they are extensions of themselves. When the partner asserts their differing opinions, the partner may interpret it as an affront.

Thus, when the partner strives to be a unique separate person, it may feel offensive to the controlling mate. These offensive abandonment feelings in an extreme case can result in physical or emotional abuse. The broken string of the painful feelings of their past neglect or abuse has been plucked.

As a result, severe disharmony in the individual and in the relationship may occur. There is an unnerving twang instead of soothing tune. Subsequently, control issues can become severely out of control. These abandonment sensitivities can become mine fields of explosive material if stepped or stomped upon.

Under the gun, one is usually too reactionary for healthy communication. One becomes too charged up to be in charge of their feelings. At this point, the emotional control issues can become out of control.

One can utilize a repertoire of ways to calm oneself and become more centered. Deep breathing is a universally effective way of calming one down as it produces more oxygen in the system. One can concentrate on one's deep breathing, and this focus can help stop one from seething.

One partner who acts out their pain often marries a partner who acts out their anguish.

Then one partner becomes a shock absorber of their partner's emotional pain. A dynamite explosion may occur when people who both act out their pain marry each other. The relationship can become emotionally and physically volatile. The escalating conflict may run out of control, resulting in a marital wreck.

This antagonistic couple may feel like relational rubble. The road of marriage cannot withstand the weight of the vehicle that is pounding the pavement. This relational pattern may be creating potholes for a bumpy, rough ride. When triggers activate painful feelings from the past that are infiltrating the present, counseling may be necessary. Counseling may be able to unravel these feelings and help the couple not to overact to their triggers.

Partners may strive to avoid stepping on triggers. When they do, they may be sensitive and not react to their partner's activated, hurtful, triggered overreactions. The couple can become trigger-happy as they control their triggers and keep them from creating an out-of-control marriage.

When a partner strives to understand the underlying pain,
The marriage has the potential of much to gain.

No one is to blame their behavior on their past. It is simply important for both partners to be sensitive to the vulnerable areas in both themselves and in their mate. Then, they will know what is happening when they are triggered, and they can understand when their spouse is triggered as well.

Couples who love each other can learn to avoid the damaging control behaviors. They can keep the anguish of one generation from infiltrating their present lives. The pattern can change, and intimacy can occur. They can give up control.

The well-known proverb is true: "If you squeeze a bird too tightly, it will die. If you let it go and it loves you, it will come back." Couples can let destructive control issues go and come together to experience a safe haven of tender loving care. When a partner becomes mad from a painful trigger and is able to keep control, the relationship can grow into something to behold. This control builds much trust, and the relationship feels safe and is unlikely to bust or rust.

Interdependence: Balancing Control

We all like to be in control. When control issues are out of control, they can ignite a damaging fire in the relationship. To put out and prevent the fires, one must at times let go of having to be in charge. The understanding of the need to let go control is enhanced by understanding interdependence. In a healthy relationship, one partner is not always in charge.

As a result, each partner's relational influence is very large. There is a difference between being independent, being dependent, and being interdependent. Moving back and forth from being independent to being dependent in a relationship is called interdependence. Being interdependent is the key to having a balance of control in a relationship.

When both partners are switching from being in control to giving the partner control, bonding is enhanced. Trust and security in a relationship is needed to relinquish control. One partner may lead in one aspect of a relationship at one time, while the other spouse may lead at another time. Both partners are influencing change agents.

When each partner takes leadership in their roles
Their partnership creates intimacy between their two souls.

Giving up the reins in a situation and then taking them in another allows both partners to take leadership roles in certain aspects of the relationship. Choosing to rotate control creates a climate for intimacy as both partners are involved in the direction of the relationship.

When one moves from no longer being single
One's life is now related to how the partners intermingle.

To help couples understand the challenges of switching roles, I have asked them to do an exercise. One partner was asked to stand while the other partner kneels in front of them. Then, they are to look at each other in the eyes. Next they let themselves feel what they feel and think what they think. Then they reverse roles.

Next, they discuss how they felt differently in each role. Couples may have positive and negative feelings in each position. When a mate is locked into a position of always having to be the strong one or being the dependent one, bonding is diminished. The strong one never, or seldom, shows vulnerability or allows the partner to give to him/her. The giving and receiving aspect of the relationship is not in tack. One person is always kneeling, while the other person is constantly standing.

In interdependence, the partner may give up control of the finances because their partner is much better at handling money. This does not mean that there is no communication regarding financial issues. It simply means that one partner provides more leadership and time concerning finances.

The couple's bond is strengthened because of the giving and receiving.

Each partner experiences receiving benefits from the other. It works because it is not against the mate's will. It is a mutual decision. The partner's feelings and integrity are intact. The spouse is being tactful regarding how the distribution of power in the relationship is handled. Then both partners do not feel like they are sitting on a tack.

Sometimes a "rescuer" personality type will marry a "dependent" personality type. The rescuer may have taken on a giving role early in life to make up for a deficient parent. The rescuer then becomes the strong one in the relationship and is constantly standing. This person has not learned to be on the receiving end. They want their partner to be the one always kneeling.

Giving up control of always being the strong one may be a difficult challenge for some accomplish. In their overzealous efforts to be strong, they may end up feeling like the victim as their own needs are not met. They then may flip into persecuting the partner for not meeting their needs. Also, when the persecuted partner tries to become strong or assume more responsibility, the rescuer may find fault in what they do in an effort to regain control. Then the cycle continues and interdependence is sabotaged.

When one person feels they always have to be the one that is strong
The relationship will end up being unhealthily wrong.

When a partner becomes tired of always being the strong one, a crisis in the relationship may result. In the danger of this crisis, there is also opportunity. The relationship has the prospect of becoming more balanced. A healthy river needs both a feeding stream and an outlet. It needs to both receive and give water. If it only gives, it will slowly become empty. If the river only receives, it will become salty like the Dead Sea, unable to sustain life.

For relationships to be healthy and enlivened, both partners must be on the giving and receiving end. Otherwise the relationship can become unable to sustain life. It may become a "Dead Sea marriage." This change requires a discussion about the relationship pattern. It may be uncomfortable to begin to change the pattern. This discomfort can be reframed as growing pains. The benefits will be priceless. The relational bond will be stronger. Instead of painful quills, feathers will be sticking out.

Communication will be more comfortable. Interdependence can

keep the relationship of giving and receiving in balance. The couple will realize that getting control issues under control matters. Interdependence gives both partners voices. No one person makes all of the choices. Communication will be rid of damaging vices, and the relationship will avoid many crises.

Conniving Control--Manipulation

Manipulation can mangle a relationship. Manipulation is a form of striving to be in control. When the partner says no and one wants them to say yes, manipulation can become a formidable weapon. This exploitation pokes at the vulnerabilities of the partner until the partner succumbs to the wishes of the manipulator.

Manipulation has many stipulations placed on one's mate. These stipulations may carry with them the marriage's fate. Exploitation creates mistrust and makes the partner cautious. If the behavior continues, the relationship may become nauseous.

The manipulator is not looking out for the well-being of their partner. The conniving behaviors are devious ploys to push the vulnerable buttons of one's partner for personal gain. These deceitful plans are implemented without regard to the partner's needs or the needs of the relationship. In some underhanded manner, the wily person may lambaste their prey until the bullied one become as silent as a lamb.

For example, manipulation occurs when a partner strives to put the other one on a guilt trip. Pushing the right button opens the door, and the partner says yes when they really want to say no. Pressuring the partner by the prick of guilt then becomes a sneaky control technique to get one's way.

One dynamic that makes a partner susceptible to manipulation is the need to please. The need to please the other partner without regard to one's own needs creates vulnerability to the trickery of manipulation. One partner allows the other partner to take what one really does not need to give. Sacrificial giving is honorable, but if sacrificial giving is a knee-jerk reaction with no thought, it can be demeaning.

There are three different kinds of doors that individual partners have in their lives. The first door is basically invisible. The partner has difficulty saying no, and the yes response to any demand is pervasive. The person then may become a doormat for the partner to trample upon. When one partner always says yes, their relationship can end up becoming a mess.

The second type of door has the doorknob on the outside. The person is sometimes able to express an appropriate no. On the other hand, at other times, the spouse intentionally pushes their partner's vulnerable button, which opens the mate's door. Then, the intruding spouse comes in and takes what their partner does not want to give. The partner has said yes when they really wanted to say no. Consequently, they feel as if they have been used.

Manipulation is used to strive to goad. If it continues, the partner may say, "Hit the road."

The manipulator strives to be the boss. Ruling by intimidation brings with it great cost.

The relationship may eventually be completely lost. Manipulation, then, can mangle the relationship.

In striving to solve the problem, the relationship can become tangled. Both partners have the responsibility to change this pattern. Respect is the key to keeping control under control. One must respect one's own needs and their partner's needs. Bonding can occur when partners are mutually fulfilling the unique needs of each other. Learning to heed to the partner's need will not happen with self-focused greed.

The third type of door has the doorknob on the inside. This partner can let their yes be yes and their no be no. This is a healthy individual. Ideally, it is good to have two partners with doorknobs on the inside. Then the control issues are under control. Each partner has the freedom to say yes and no and will not allow the other to manipulate them into usurping their own autonomy.

Learning how to be assertive and not aggressive gives respect to the wishes of the partner, while one strives to fulfill one's own needs. Learning one's rights and respecting the rights of their partner sets the stage for true intimacy. Thus, assertive communication has no room for manipulation. Assertiveness will knock on the door and accept a yes or a no. There will be no intruding into the life of the partner without permission. They are expressing their preferences and not raising the request to the level of a daunting demand.

When each partner can accept a yes or a no
The warmth of the relationship climate helps the couple to grow.

Aggressive behavior runs roughshod over the rights of the partner. Then their constitutional rights to "life, liberty, and the pursuit of happiness" have been violated. Democracy cannot be enjoyed in the home. Tyrannical behavior raises its ugly head. Only one vote counts. The voices of both are not heard in the process of decision-making. An equal rights, proclaimed by the constitution, do not move from the country into the four walls of the home.

The following is an example of an unhealthy way and a healthy way of relating: For the most part, asking with an attitude of preference instead of a demand can create a win-win. A demand puts much tension in communication and makes it difficult to withstand. A power struggle can begin, and it can turn into a lose-lose relationship.

Of course, behaviors can be so extreme that they cannot be tolerated. If this behavior continues, the bond will be broken or greatly abated. A behavior that is so damaging is not open to be debated. It will sabotage the bond that has been created. These are behaviors that can be demanded to be stopped. In general, demanding does not produce a needed dialogue, which is at the heart of a healthy relationship.

In the first interchange, a suggestion is to be accepted without question. This demand can create relational indigestion.

Spouse 1: "We are going to move to California when school is out."
Spouse 2: "Can't we discuss this matter? The move would set me back greatly in my career. I have worked hard to advance and get a job that is very fulfilling."
Spouse 1: "We are going to move to California because I want to be near my family. There will be no discussion regarding this matter. You put your career above my needs. That is despicable."
Spouse 2: "I just want to discuss the decision. Can we wait until I see what kind of job I can find there?"
Spouse 1: "No, I can find a job anywhere in the medical field. I can support the family. You do not even need to work. I am going to set up the arrangements for the moving van to come next week. You get to packing, or our relationship will be totally lacking. If you do not come along, we can call it quits. I will not tolerate your fits."

Only one voice counted. The voice of the other spouse was not taken in consideration. Here is a more productive alternative scenario.

This couple avoided caustic communication, creating disillusion
By listening to each other, they began to move toward resolution.

Spouse 1: "I am missing my family and friends. I would like to move to California and be near them. What do you think?"

Spouse 2: "Honey, moving would be very difficult for me. I have worked hard to get a job that I like, and the advancement in my career has been a long time coming. I am also concerned that living so close to your family could have a negative impact on our relationship."

Spouse 1: "There are two concerns that you have about the move. You are concerned about how it would affect your career. You are also concerned about how living close to my family would affect our relationship."

Spouse 2: "Yes, it would be very difficult for me to get a job in my field at the same level in your hometown. Also, when we lived with your family before, you spent so much time with them that we had little time for ourselves. They came over often and without even calling. Also, you went to visit them almost every weekend."

Spouse 1: "What ideas do you have? Do you think that we can have a compromise?"

Spouse 2: "Yes, if we moved to the big city 80 miles from your family, I think I could find a good job there. Also, having some distance could help us to set better boundaries between our relationship and your family."

Spouse 1: "I see what you mean. I think we should put more thought in this decision."

Spouse 2: "We can spend time looking at this and other options over the next months and see if we can come to some mutual agreement."

Spouse: "I like that idea."

Both voices were heard and there was openness to dialogue. Respect for both partner's feelings was demonstrated. The couple is on their way to finding a solution that will satisfy both. There was wisdom in the discussion. Serenity, wisdom, and calmness prevailed. They are exploring what can be changed without having a negative impact. Also, in the pursuing discussion, each partner may consider what should not be changed or what cannot be changed.

It is evident then that there needs to be a declaration of interdependence in the family, which allows freedom to ring over our land and into the hearts and lives of our families. The liberty bell then has meaning for families. Control issues become under control. Spouses will matter to each other, and their relationship will matter.

Bonding need not use superglue, resulting in no separateness in the couple's togetherness. It should be more like a flexible adhesive. The bond is there, but the couple is not stuck together. This ability to make this kind of relationship work is dependent upon emotional safety. This kind of relational safety occurs when each partner feels respected and admired, and the partner is out for their mate's well-being. Trust is the glue that produces this bond. Trust can also be the balm of healing when there are failures regarding the goal of producing intimacy.

Being sensitive to the painful partner's wounds can build a strong bond very soon.

Relational coping strategies are paramount in moving forward toward your purpose, passion, and excellence. You will look at your goals and not engage in avoidance. Your focus will remain steady as you encounter an annoyance. Your creativity will overcome obstacles with brilliance. Your diligence will move you through a disturbance. Your emotions will remain in balance. You will need autonomy in great amount. Your inner wisdom you will not discount. Your relationship with yourself needs to be fundamentally sound. This sense of self will help you keep your feet on the ground.

CHAPTER 8

Following Through Can Ignite a Breakthrough

Good intentions are a good start.
Following through is what enables you to hit the mark.

—Dan Crenshaw

I F YOU ARE going to experience transformation and grow creatively from grief to greatness, your life needs to have proper formation. When the basic form of the strategy is set, a follow-through needs to occur for goals to be met. With continued procrastination, you cannot wallow through. Taking the first step is the key to your breakthrough. Tomorrow will never come. Today is the time to act or your breakthrough will remain mum.

Without action, you will never find a crumb. With transformation out of formation, no compass will guide the way. You will be in the dark and there you will stay. The lighthouse will have lost its beam. Excellence, purpose, and passion will not be seen. A follow-through can be guided by your core values. These values with a sense of purpose can keep you from the blues.

Your life will begin to surge as your attitude renews. Your emotions will be sturdy and not sing the blues. You will not be in neutral as you shift to a high gear. You will follow through with meaning that you hold so dear. You will be bold and overcome any fear. As the gears of your life take a shift, you will no longer linger and drift. You will see the target on the scope, and it will be in sight. The dawn of a new day is beginning, and your actions will not be trite. You will enjoy the journey with immense delight.

Being Unreasonably Reasonable Can Ignite a Breakthrough.

Being unreasonably reasonable goes beyond the seemingly possible. It is making possible what only appears impossible. It turns extraordinary dreams into reality by empowering you to become the big person that you are in actuality. You can analyze a goal to death. Making a decision that is not rational provides energizing breath. Your hope will enable you to see your enormous capacity. You will find that you are bigger than the challenging activity.

You will develop the courage to gain a vision that will stretch your mission. Being unreasonable granted you hope to make a life-changing decision. It goes against the grain of ordinary, reasonable thought. You can reach goals that you would not have wrought. Being unreasonably reasonable makes you virtually invincible. This attitude inspires you to go beyond what is ordinarily sensible.

People will become inspired and want to be a part of your adventure. They will not limit their thoughts by inappropriate censure. Taking action on what is unreasonably reasonable will not always succeed. But taking action on many goals that are unreasonably will reap rewards indeed. The courage that you develop by being unreasonably reasonable will make many things possible that were previously thought unfeasible.

You can analyze a goal to death. Making a decision that is not rational provides energizing breath. Your hope will enable you to see your enormous capacity. You will find that you are bigger than the needed activity. Having an unreasonable reasonable outlook can inspire others to take steps they have never took. You can see in their face that they have a different look. What are unreasonable actions that you can make today? Commitment can become a catalyst to spark you on your way.

Your life will be as different as night is today. The light will dawn, and you will find your way.

Values bring fuel for the fire. You will no longer be frustrated and filled with ire. Following through with purpose, passion, and excellence with become a habit. You will no longer be wasting time aimlessly chasing a rabbit.

If you are going to experience transformation, your life needs to have proper formation. The basic strategy is set. As you begin your journey, your mind can feel that you have reached your destination. This state of mind will shift your life to a beautiful transformation.

Transformation: Follow Through by Leaning into Your Dreams.

Leaning into an uphill run makes running much more efficient and fun. You will be proud of yourself when your race is done. Leaning into your dreams helps you to keep your stride. Leaning away from your dreams may result in a rough ride. When you lean forward when someone is talking, you are more alert. When you lean toward a dream, your focus will not divert. Leaning into your dreams can surface a well-planned scheme. Leaning into your dreams can help the possibilities of your dreams to be seen.

Leaning away from your dreams cay lead you astray. You never will find if there is a possible way. Your life will be unstable, and you are likely to fall. It may feel like your dreams have hit a wailing wall. Leaning forward helps you to assert their most efficient actions. In leaning backward, one can only have hapless reactions. Leaning forward will serve as a bridge to go over any obstacle. Leaning backward will only result in a debacle.

When you lean forward when someone is talking, you are more alert. When you lean forward into a dream your focus will not divert. Leaning into your dreams can surface a well-planned scheme. Leaning into your dreams can help the possibility of your dreams to be seen. When you lean away from your dreams, they do not come to reality. The final destination of the dream can feel like a fatality. Leaning into your dreams can inspire others to follow. When you lean away from your dreams, you can only wallow.

Inspiring others to follow can provide much more momentum. People working together toward a dream can prevent a conundrum. The eye of the hurricane is calm. When you lean onto life, it can be a balm. When you lean forward when someone is talking you are more alert. When you lean forward into a dream your focus will not divert.

Leaning into your dreams can surface a well-planned scheme. Leaning into your dreams can help the possibly of your dreams to be seen. When you lean backward, opportunities can pass you by. Not being in a position to take the opportunity could make you cry. Leaning forward one can help you seize the moment. Then opportunities can be taken, warding off torment. When you lean forward, your life is more stable. As you deal with what shows up in life, you are more able. When you lean backward, your life will be filled with instability. Leaning backward creates a feeling of having a disability.

When you lean forward, your dream journey can take a lunge. When you lean backward, your dreams may take a plunge. When you lean backward, your dreams may feel like grunge. When leaning forward, the fear of failure you will expunge. When you lean forward when someone is talking you are more alert. When you lean forward into a dream your focus will not divert. Leaning into your dreams can surface a well planned scheme. Leaning into your dreams can result your dreams to be seen.

Your resulting transformation can result in an artistic sensation. When you are working creatively, you feel like you are on vacation. Your transformation will come from a thrilling, heartfelt emancipation. You feel in your heart that you have already reached in your destination.

The journey then becomes exciting with no procrastination. The vibrations of the passion and creativity of your heart are filled with inspiration. The words that you say to yourself are encouraging words of affirmation. Others see you differently and are filled with admiration.

As you continue your journey of leaning into your dreams, you can experience adoration. You are leaning fully into your dreams with full activation. You are excited to fulfill your heart's deepest aspiration. You are charismatic, magnetic, and full of animation.

You are in a creative process of cultivation. You are already beginning to feel a sense of celebration. You know that you will reach your destination. Leaning into your dreams have begun substantive germination.

You are increasing your momentum and your creative dream's inclination. You mind is focused and alert with the full present moment in peaceful concentration. The journey is filled with elation, and you have no hesitation. You heart, mind, and spirit are in harmony as you move toward your dream's realization. People around you are picking up on your positive vibrations and enhancing your stimulation. Your heart, mind, and soul are filled with a feeling of titillation. There is no room in your heart for trepidation. You are on a focused journey with no vacillation.

Your life has taken a shift, and you are in a mindset of transformation. You have a mission to accomplish with vision, imagination, and visualization. You know what your destiny looks like, and you are filled with motivation. You sense deeply your possibilities and are not concerned about any limitation. As you are filled with a vision of your creative dream, you are utilizing improvisation.

You are filled with a since of purpose, passion, and edification. You know that when your dreams are manifested, you will be experiencing much solicitation. Leaning into your dreams already creates a sense of validation. If you leaned away from your dreams, you would experience a sense of hopeless desperation. If you leaned away from your dreams, you would experience immobilization. When moving toward your dreams, you feel a sense of acceleration. You have declared your freedom in this exciting embarkation.

You are feeling an increasing sense of dedication. You have done your preparation. Now you have a great expectation. The seeds of germination are beginning to bud and blossom with artful beautification. As you are leaving forward into your dreams, you have no sense of hesitation. You are moving out of your shift of transformation and restoration. You are demonstrating your freedom of manifestation and declaration. You are being fueled by a powerful aspiration.

This follow-through to transformation is no aberration. It is embedded deeply in your heart's liberation. You are beautifully in charge of your dream's orchestration. The journey within itself is filled with jubilation. Leaning backward, you would feel a sense of intimidation. Leaning forward, you experience your possibilities and not your limitation.

Follow Through by Getting Out of Your Own Way.

By getting out of your own way, your continued growth will be here to stay. If a dragon attempts to get in your way, you will slay. Growth is natural under the right conditions. Being in your own corner will free ambitions from inhibitions. You can feel your own power as it becomes your friend. It is power that is good for you and others, resulting in a win-win. Getting out of your own way can then become the onset of peace within. You know that you deserve success, and you cannot wait to begin.

You will attract others with your positive energy. Like a rolling snowball, the momentum will accelerate with resulting synergy. Frosty the Snowman will go over the hills of snow. The journey will expand your vision, and you will be in the know. Your wisdom, serenity, and courage will build as confidence becomes strong. You may have been waiting for this level of confidence for very long. One can indeed celebrate life like a beautifully singing bird. The tangible results can also reap intangible rewards that go beyond any word.

The expression on your face leaves no doubt regarding your inner passion. You will not feel that your creative energies will have to be under ration. Your bountiful energy will be set free in a remarkably efficient action. Any opposition will not result in a retraction. This passion will fuel your life to move through obstacles.

Negativity will not let the air out of the tires. One's attitude will keep passionate, burning fires. By getting out of your own way, your continued growth will be here to stay. Growth is natural for all living things under the right conditions. Being in your own corner will free your ambitions from inhibitions.

Following Through with a Routine Does Not Have to be Routine.

A routine can become a daily habit that helps your mind stay focused and keen. You do not have to think about how to keep your house in order. You just go through the flow to prevent clutter and disorder. A routine can become a good habit. It helps you from becoming mentally scattered and chasing a rabbit. It can keep bad habits and thoughts from finding space in your life to inhabit. Then you will have the energy when an opportunity arises to grab it.

Also, if grief or loss comes your way, you have the energy to use coping skills to keep grief from finding a home to stay. You can do grief work that interrupts your life because your house is in order and you have a reserve of energy for strife. Good habits can keep you from chasing after rabbits. Good habits can empower you to hit your targets. Good habits can ward off life's difficult bullets. Good habits can enhance assists and prevent debits.

By having good habits, you will be empowered to be acknowledged by many credits. Good habits can enable you to evaluate all facets. Good habits can help you to be one of the favorites. Good habits will prevent you from experiencing forfeits. Good habits will help you to handle any obstacles and culprits.

With good habits, you will not be a person who nervously fidgets. Good habits will give you more possibilities and fewer limits. Good habits will provide you with many merits. Good habits will bring you many kinds of profits. Good habits will prevent you from having embarrassing secrets. Good habits will attract opportunities like magnets.

A solid routine can help your life to become more pristine. A solid routine can be creatively keen. A solid routine can help you to be more serene. A solid routine can help make your coping muscles leaner. A solid routine can create possibilities in the future that are presently unseen. A solid routine can become like energizing, nutritious protein.

A solid routine can help you create a bridge over a life-challenging ravine. A solid routine can keep the bugs out of your life like a windscreen. A solid routine can produce results that have not been previously seen. A solid routine can help a toxic environment like a shot of vaccine.

A routine can represent your priorities. You can become your final authority. You are the executive of your life's direction. A solid routine of habits can give balance and lessen the need for correction. Your core values will become virtually automatic, and a routine can keep you less stressed as you live in the present moment.

Your body will be better able to ward off a possible ailment. You will not be so drained that your talents will lie dormant. A routine can become a stress treatment. A routine can become a part of your core values and not just a valueless fragment.

Encroachments won't feel like your head has just hit the pavement. Routine and good habits can provide a healing ointment. Your life will be more focused and valiant. You will know what needs to be done and what can be left for another time. You will know what behaviors are not worth a dime. A good routine and habits can increase your self-esteem. You will experience the value of what routine and habits can mean. A routine is not boring, as on the surface it may seem. It can give you energy for inspiration to fashion a life scheme.

A routine can make your life efficient and buoyant. You can see that with focused energy, you can be brilliant. Regarding reaching purpose, passion, and excellence, you will be content. With less stress, you are less apt to be errant. You will be much more fervent. With having good priorities, you will not seem flippant.

Your life will surge toward forward moment. You can be powerfully tactful and not become reactively blunt. You will have more strength to appropriately confront. You will be more apt to keep your responsibilities current. Procrastination will not be a tyrant. Your strengths will be in the forefront. Your errors will be less flagrant. You will feel that you are respectful and decent.

By becoming more organized with routine, you can find things you need in an instant. You will not be as apt to lose things and have to go on an anxious hunt. Keeping things in order will help prevent others responding with an affront. You will gain more of an attraction from others as you are prudent.

You will not accept someone talking to you in nonmilitary life like a sergeant. You will be gracious to others when necessary and be appropriately poignant. Your follow-through in life will be brilliant. Your attitude will be ardent. You will find that as you follow through, your life will be less errant. You will not be stagnant. You will be potent.

Following through by Clearing out Clutter

You can grip the gavel and bang and exclaim, "Let there be order in the house!" Uttering against cluttering is more than muttering. It is emphatically recognizing a habit that increases stress and suffering. Uttering against cluttering can keep your life from sputtering. Clutter squeezes out the room to create. The expression of the heart is not artful but an ache. When clutter is cleared, creation will have already appeared. There is space for new clothes, new ideas, and new actions. Your environment and your life will have multifaceted attractions.

With empowerment surging from within, you cannot wait to begin. You embark, sparked by a creative urge. Your mind, body, and spirit will merge. A shift and transformation will emerge. The tripod will work in tandem to create possibilities for the future for sure. Your countenance is attracting people with your allure. What before seemed like wishful thinking is now flowing smoothly, clearing out any kinking. It is like a magical potion that you have been drinking. It provides miraculous changes in your feelings, behavior, and thinking. The people around you will fill your positive vibes. Some will support you with loyalty that continuously abides. You will have a kick in your step and increase the length of your strides.

The mind can have space to create and not be cluttered, creating a mental logjam. Then the creative ideas can flow and keep you on the go and not scram. When you open a closet with clutter, a mess may unfold. Your spirit, mind, and emotions need a clearing for new ideas to uphold. When you express every random thought that comes to your mind, communication is cluttered and is not effective, and you waste time. You will become more efficient and use language that empowers your mind.

Good thoughts lead to good behavior and motivation. Your lifestyle will lead to a vibrant inner ovation. You will no longer utter clutter resulting in meaningless mutter. Clearing the clutter in your mind can lead to a chaotic thinking's demise. As order becomes a habit, your energy will rise.

Your potential for purpose, passion, and excellence can soar to the skies. With mental clutter gone, your lifestyle will not be erratic. Clearing out the clutter can stop distracting mental and emotional static. Your voice will be productively and clearly emphatic. Your life can become filled with excellence that is extraordinarily dynamic.

Following through by Having an Anchor, Not Rancor

An anchor holds us down securely. Rancor rails away with anger insecurely. An anchor helps a person feel that his life is on solid ground. Rancor manifests itself like a howling hound. When an anchor is released, it sets a person free to venture forward. Rancor can result in a person's life going wayward. An anchor can help one's life to go upward. Rancor can make one's life feel like one is in a blinding blizzard. An anchor can help one to survive a vicious storm. Rancor can be the source of a relationship being torn. An anchor can provide cement where a pole can stand.

Rancor can become more like quicksand. A person who is anchored can have much character. A person with rancor has no anchor. Cynicism cannot result in an attitude that attracts success. An anchor can attract others for networking, resulting in your best. An anchor can be a point in which one can move forward. Rancor can keep one stuck in a position that is awkward. Core values habitually followed can keep your life in proper balance. A sense of purpose can help one to keep rancor in silence.

Following through Ignited by Possibility Thinking

Does it seem like you would have to leap the Grand Canyon to move from where you are to where you would like to be? Someone asked for directions. The response was that you cannot get there from here. The question is raised: "What kind of place do you need to be in your mind, heart, and spirit to get there from here?" That place is having the attitudinal stance that will propel you across the chasm.

The successful outcome comes out of possibility thinking. What is possible regarding where you are and where you can go? This chasm can be narrowed by possibility thinking instead of limited thinking. Enlarging your options can decrease the gap between where you are and where you would like to be. You can reach the other side of the Grand Canyon and experience a grand life.

The distance between where you are and where you would like to be is not as large as you might think.

It is worth repeating the story of the boy whose 300-pound granddad was on top of him on the bed. The little boy wanted to be on top of his granddad. He began to gain a vision. *I am on top of you in my mind.* Gaining a purpose, passion, mission, and vision can help you to cope with obstacles and be on top of things in your mind. Then you will not mind doing what is necessary to continue.

Accepting yourself regarding where you are can give you the serenity and peace to reduce your stress and give you momentum to help you go on a journey toward your purposeful destination and decrease the chasm between where you are and where you want to be. Having the attitude and feeling that you are already there creates behaviors, thoughts, feelings, and attitudes that will empower you to enlarge your horizon and enter the grand life over what no longer seems like the Grand Canyon.

You are on top of the challenge in your mind. There is a swelling of confidence and a kick in your step that will produce a forward march. You can become energized to do more than you previously thought was possible. What you had to accept that you could not change has turned into something that you can change. You have taken an emotional, athletic stance so you can move more efficiently toward your newly discovered possibilities.

The blinds were raised, and the sunshine was let in. You will be able to accept what you cannot change and begin to enlarge the possibilities of what you can change. A shift has occurred and put the care of your life into another gear, and you found that you had more power to move along down the journey of life. Momentum increased as it seemed that you were going downhill instead of up a treacherous climb up the mountain.

There is a purpose for a diving board. It becomes a springboard for divers to spring up into the air to accomplish many maneuvers before they dive into the water. Then enter the water without making a splash. You can dive into life and enter the water of life more smoothly. You will not belly bust and experience needless pain as you go more deeply into your potential.

There may be growing pains as you step out of your comfort zone, but the pain will not make you groan or moan. Your life will be in tune, making musical tones. You will experience a restoration to propel you to chime in and reach your destination. Possibilities emerge quicker out of a mood that is light. Music can lighten your mood and help your efforts to be skillful and not crude.

I have taken acting lessons and found out that the potential I had in acting was greater than I thought it to be. I have taken fitness training and found that my potential for fitness was greater than I had envisioned. My body has taken on a new shape. Creating a total life design is a culmination of utilizing the previously mentioned coping skills that were strengthened in the challenging grief journey and applied to your life in general.

They are linked together, and one feeds off on the other. Together they can have a powerful influence on your life in terms of growing toward purpose, passion, and excellence. These coping mechanisms culminate into a powerful foundation for a total life design. The winds of life can huff and puff but not blow your house down. When one area of life strengthens, it can help strengthen another part. Strengthening you physique can help your confidence, undergirding a solid coping skill. Your potential in other areas of your life can be enhanced as stress is down and doing your is up.

Your strengthened energy will help you to be less vulnerable emotionally. You will cope with conflict and the normally depleting, stressful aspects of life. You will have more freedom to choose your battles and conserve energy. You will be able to stay on course with the ship of your life. You compass will be more accurate, sending you toward the right direction. Your lighthouse can help you to find direction when your life is filled with darkness. Healthy family relations can become a haven to help you to have more energy to go forward with you head high in the world.

Following through by Living in the Powerful Now

A significant part of pet loss is the opportunity to begin to incorporate in your total life design the total life cycle of life and death. When most of our population raised cattle and farm animals, they were more accustomed as life and death became a natural part of the total life design. Death is a more foreign, emotional language for us to deal with.

There is a sense in which when we learn how to come to terms with this part of our life cycle, we can live life more fully. There is an anonymous story about a Zen master who was dying. His students were around him.

They cherished each moment in his presence. He said that he would like to have a piece of chocolate cake.

One of the students brought back a gourmet chocolate cake and cut him a slice. He picked up his fork and put a morsel of the cake in his mouth. Then his strength began to wane as he dropped his fork. They exclaimed, "Zen Master! Zen Master! Give us your last words of wisdom." He exclaimed, "My was that cake delicious." In effect, his last words of wisdom were to live until you die. He had come to terms with death.

We can eradicate the pain of grief and dying. It can help us cope more effectively to add to the quality of life that we live. I used to lead conferences on death and dying, and one of the ten questions that I asked the classes to ponder was, "If you knew that you had only six months of life to live, how would you live it?"

This can bring our priorities from the background into the foreground. We can activate our priorities when we bring to the fore the brevity of life. This is not morbid thinking. It is a kind of thinking that helps us to squeeze all of the juice out of the orange of life. Life can become fuller and tastier. We can live in the present moment and say, "My, my life is delicious."

Life is lived more peacefully in the moment. Dogs and animals naturally live life in the moment. They can teach us many aspects of life that can increase the quality of our life. To the degree that we can develop unconditional love to others and ourselves is the strength that we can have to wash away much of the toxic feelings of resentment, anger, and rancor, which can take much of the air out of our tires. This wasted energy can leave us with a flat life.

Living in the present moment can maximize your effectiveness in utilizing the coping mechanisms needed for effective living. We can gain them from our bonding with our pets during their lives, and we can gain as we learn to cope with the painful loss and changes dealing with their death. These coping mechanisms culminate into a powerful foundation for a total life design. The winds of life cannot "huff and puff but not blow your house down."

I have taking fitness training, which emphasizes many muscle groups. I am exercising my arms more than any other muscle. Parts of my body are being left out. My body strength is not in balance. A lifestyle of utilizing creative coping skills can work on all the muscle groups of your life and grant you a total life design. It feels great to be developing my body where the total body feels fit and equally fit. Then your body is less likely to give you a fit. As they become strong, they culminate in a total lifestyle that can move one toward purpose, passion, and excellence. The options and possibilities of life expand. Meaning is enhanced. They feed off each other to gain powerful nutrition to develop a full body experience fitness that can continue its power and growth for the rest of your life.

Attitudes, behavior, emotions, and relationships will create muscles that can invigorate your whole system. All of your coping muscles can be developed and enhanced. It can help you to expand all of the muscles of your coping life. Your whole lifestyle can move toward greater purpose, passion, and excellence.

With core values at the center, aspects of life include:

1. Healthy self-care
2. Social fun
3. Personal and spiritual development
4. Physical environment
5. Career/life purpose
6. Family and friends/community
7. Finances
8. Romance and intimacy

To the degree that these eight major aspects of life are not actuated is the degree that you are behind the eight ball. You are hindering yourself from moving forward in life. How do you eat an elephant? You eat it one bite at a time. Making small steps can increase the quality of your life to enormous depths. Recognize the progress and you will not regress. Your motivation will increase, and you will have a key to life's access.

The result of utilizing the coping mechanism together can help create a total life design that leads toward purpose, passion, and excellence in every area of your life. It can help you to make significant strides in these areas. The coping skills needed to journey through grief are largely basic coping skills that you need to effectively journey through life.

It copes with challenges on the way to successful living. The coping skills that fuel grief and enable grief work to work are the same coping skills that enable a person to ignite the spark plugs of life. These coping skills enable the engine of life to start quickly and to run efficiently.

Follow Through by Adjusting to Encroachments.

Unwanted encroachments can spark creative adjustments. These adjustments can refine, strengthen and add to your repertoire of coping skills. Unexpected encroachments can lead to reproach. When they come it is vital to have a coping approach. Unexpected accidents and losses can be difficult to bear. No one desires such events to happen that can create an unknown future scare.

You can creatively and courageously respond to unexpected life encroachments, which few people would ever dare. It is hope that can inspire you to adjust with wisdom that is priceless and rare. These painful encroachments may thwart a previous goal. But the scenario that ensues can become a creative journey as one watches it unfold. It can be an inspiration to others as they find a character that is bold. Then the encroachment will not feel like a circumstance of life that was out to scold.

Unexpected accidents and can indeed be difficult to bear. The fabric of your life may feel like it has an irreparable tear. But the fabric of your life does not have to feel torn. New, creative possibilities for the future can be born. You will avoid feeling forlorn. What shows up in life can create incredibly painful strife.

One may feel temporarily stunned and dead, but one can come back to life free of dread. By diving back into the world, one can discover creative ways to deal with the cards that one has been dealt. This creative behavior can bring one exciting results You can ignite transformational breakthroughs by fervently following through. What is really you can become true. With motivation, you can set yourself apart. You can move toward purpose, passion, and excellence and inspire others to have a transformational start. Now you are ready to fully embark. You are destined to make your mark.

CHAPTER 9

Motivational Rap Rhapsodies: Poetic Rhyme with a Heartbeat

UTILIZING THE RAP format and fertilizing it with positive life nutrients can transform it into a positive art form. Facing reality and letting go needs the following character traits.

Grow from your grief journey and become monumentally great.

The titles of the rap lyrics are as follows:

1. Rap Has Been Given a Bad Rap
2. Patience Brings Prudence
3. Living in the Mean Time
4. Look Out for Your Outlook
5. Being Perfectly Imperfect
6. Good Habits Prevent Chasing Rabbits
7. Doggone It, My Dog Is Gone
8. From Grief to Greatness
9. Leaning into Your Dreams
10. Taming Shame
11. It's Mean Not to Give Life Meaning
12. Prevent Messing with Stressing

1. Rap Has Been Given a Bad Rap
Dan C. Crenshaw

Chorus

Rap has been given a bad rap.
This art form has not been used to collect the tree of life's sap.
Rap can motivate the body, mind, and soul.
Rap can keep one's heart from growing old.

Verse 1

Motivational rap can use an artistic brush
To prevent the need to tell rap to hush.
Rap can tap you on the shoulder and make you become bolder.
Rap can be for the baby boomers.
Rap can help people of all ages to become bloomers.
This is the potential that rap has to offer.
And I am going to explore this medium before I go to the coffer.
My writing, speaking, acting, and poetic gifts
Can keep many people from getting into rifts.
I can speak to draining matters of life.
And keep people from succumbing to strife.
Rap can motivate the soul.
The rewards can create stories yet untold.
You can mine the gold that is inside.
You will enhance a healthy sense of pride.
No talent will be able to hide.

Chorus

Rap has been given a bad rap.
This art form has not been fully used to collect the tree of life's sap.
Rap can motivate the body, mind, and soul.
Rap can keep one's heart from ever growing old.

Verse 2

Instead of allowing oneself to get stuck and suffer,
Rapping can be more than a buffer.
It can buff the body, soul, and mind
And create a life that has a diamond-like shine.
I am no longer going to give rap a bad rap.
Motivational rapping has the potential to fill a huge gap.
Rap does not have to be cynical, demeaning, and obscene.
Rap does not have to be a smokescreen hiding what one life can really
mean.
Rap does not have to stop.

Motivational rap can help your cream to rise to the top.
Rap can motivate people and free them from life's being a dread.
Motivational rap can help people get ahead.
Can rap become a part of my life-coaching career?
It is a dream that could become a goal of good cheer.
That is a question that is a part of my journey's quest.
To see what my dreams will become before I come to rest.

Chorus

Rap has been given a bad rap.
This art form has not been fully used to collect the tree of life's sap.
Rap can motivate the body, mind, and soul.
Rap can keep one's heart from ever growing old.

Verse 3

You have talents that are yet undiscovered.
You have a challenge to bring them to light and allow them to be uncovered.
Who knows what talents are latent in your mind?
Not to allow them to surface and develop would be a crime.
Will you allow more and more of your talents to be released?
I believe you will, and your service to humankind will increase.
Your thirst for your hidden talents will never cease.
You will mine the gold that is inside.
You will enhance a healthy sense of pride.
No talent will be able to hide.
Your talents will continue to surface and abide.
Will I become a life coach rapper?
I will not allow negativity to become a zapper.
Being a motivational rapper could even become dapper.
Some may call me Rapper Dapper Dan
You are the man.

Chorus

Let the possibilities begin
Allow negativity to end
You have a precious life to spend.
Cash in your talents and reap the rewards.
Courage will prevail and overcome inner cowards.
A motivational rap can become a life rhapsody that is not blue.
It can inspire what is genuinely you to become true.
You can have a transformational breakthrough

2. Patience Brings Prudence

Dan Crenshaw

Chorus

Patience can grant a keen conscience as you live in the present.
Patience can help you to bathe your life in its essence.
Patience will give you a glowing countenance.
Patience will give you a hero's semblance

Verse 1

Patience is not avoidance.
Patience can allow you to stare life in the face
And avoid a negligent consequence.
Patience is not a hindrance.
Patience can bring balance.
The ability to be patient can surface in silence.
Creative coping can bring healing within your grasp.
Coping with grief with patience can aid in this arduous task.
Patience can aid in enjoying the journey and reaching your goal at last.
Patience can bring clarity and guidance.
You can be kind to yourself and experience a healing, attitudinal stance.
Patience can prevent vengeance.
Patience promotes endurance.
Patience brings serenity and assurance.
Patience will not allow obstinate defiance.
Patience will grant your goals allowance.

Chorus

Patience can grant a keen conscience as you live in the present.
Patience can help you to bathe your life in its essence.
Patience will give you a glowing countenance.
Patience will give you a hero's semblance.

Verse 2

Patience fosters persistence.
You will persist, and any grief will subside and barely exist.
Patience can bring healthy periods of calm silence.
You can be by yourself and not depend on others as your sole reliance.
You will move through anger and not feel continual defiance.
Patience can be healings essence.
You can live with the pain and not get caught up in the consequences of avoidance.
You can have the time to go inward and outward for guidance.
As a result, your life will have more substance.
You will be less apt to experience wanting vengeance.
You will have the patience for thorough, due diligence.
Patience will give you common sense in abundance.
Patience will provide you with the character of reliance.
Patience will allow your life to be full of sustenance.
You life will have a unique cadence with patience.
With patience, you will feel that challenges and obstacles are not a hindrance.

Chorus

Patience can grant a keen conscience as you live in the present.
Patience can help you to bathe your life in its essence.
Patience will give you a glowing countenance.
Patience will give you a hero's semblance

3. Living in the Meantime
Dan C. Crenshaw

Chorus

Living in the meantime does not have to seem like a brutal imposition.
Creatively coping with change can gradually put you in a better position.
Living in the meantime can seem mean.
With support beyond grief, a renewed life can reign supreme.

Verse 1

You may have lost control regarding circumstances that erupt.
Living in the meantime does not have to be a mean time that can totally disrupt.
Living in the meantime can become an adventure.
You will become free to explore new opportunities and places to venture.
You do not have to feel lost.
The mean time does not have to be a great cost.
You can explore paths for a new dream.
Living in the meantime can be a time to be serene.
The meantime does not have to be a time when you hear a siren.
Transitions can be a time to find experiences of life that taste like cream.
Living in the meantime does not have to feel like inertia and resistance.
Living in this time of transition can summon growth, creativity, and persistence.
Living in the meantime can feel like a damper,
You may feel afraid and want to scamper.
Brainstorming can take one's brain out of the storm.
Brainstorming can create new ideas that go beyond the norm.

Chorus

Living in the meantime does not have to seem like a brutal imposition.
Creatively coping with change can gradually put you in a better disposition.
Living in the meantime can seem mean.
With support beyond grief, a renewed life can reign supreme.

Verse 2

When you gain a new perspective, transitions do not have to be mean.
A new and different life can emerge, and the change is not what it may seem.
You will not have to feel stuck in the muck of a bad dream.
You can take action with emotional and spiritual muscles being lean.
Living in the meantime can become a mean time.
You are in a difficult transition and do not feel like a dime.
Living in the meantime you can feel a loss.

This time of transition can become a boss.
You may have lost control regarding circumstances that erupt.
Living in the meantime does not have to be a mean time that can totally disrupt.
Living in the meantime can become an adventure.
You will become free to explore new opportunities and places to venture.
You can commit yourself to growth and take a strong stand.
You can venture on a journey that inspires others and become in great demand.
Others that are going through a mean time can gain inspiration and hope.
They can feel strong and wise instead of wanting to mope.

Chorus

Living in the meantime does not have to seem like a brutal imposition.
Creatively coping with change can gradually put you in a better position.
With support, beyond grief a renewed life can reign supreme.
With support, beyond grief a renewed live can reign supreme.

4. Look Out for Your Outlook
Dan C. Crenshaw

Chorus

Look out for your outlook.
Your ventures will make it appear that you are a schnook.
An extraordinary outlook needs a journey within.
Looking inward is a foundation for looking outward to begin.

Verse 1

Looking out for your outlook
Necessitates that you take a second look.
What is there to be improved, added, or deleted?
Looking inward can help your energy not to be needlessly depleted.
Looking out for your outlook is not just a glance.
It is looking deeply inward for transformation to have a chance.

Blind spots are found and brought to light.
Changes are made, as looking inward will grant you more insight.
You can live a life that will give you fulfillment and delight.
Journeying inward can help you to venture out with purposeful actions
Which will provide additions to others' lives instead of subtractions.
Life can be about others, as you have taken care of your needs.
You will have the energy to support others when their heart bleeds.
You will be able to reach out to the community and beyond
And make the world a better place for goodness to spawn.
Taking a stand for another's excellence can be mutually beneficial.

Chorus

Look out for your outlook.
Your ventures and responses will not be shook.
An extraordinary outlook needs a journey within.
Looking inward is a foundation for looking outward to begin.

Verse 2

Your eyes will be looking out for a mission to accomplish.
Your actions can provide inspiration for others to flourish.
Your behavior and decisions will cause obstacles to vanish.
Then you can move to help heal others who are experiencing anguish.
Their minds, hearts, and spirits will no longer be famished.
Looking within will transform their outlook, and they will not languish.
They will become inspired and live a life that they cherish.
The flavor of their lives will increase as it adds garnish.
Their vision will become clear, and their hope will not tarnish.
What they will accomplish will astonish.
They will do no self-talk that will admonish.
Their mind will be clear and not full of gibberish.
You will know what your mind and heart wish.
Your goal will not be the big fish that got away.
Your focus will be steady and will not sway.
You will excel as you consistently pray.

Chorus

Look out for your outlook.
Your ventures and responses will not be shook.
An extraordinary outlook needs a journey within.
Looking inward is a foundation for looking outward to begin.

5. Being Perfectly Imperfect
Dan C. Crenshaw

Chorus

Being perfectly imperfect allows mistakes to become stepping stones.
When someone has to be perfect, you may hear many moans.
Perfectionism is a tyrant that paralyzes with fear.
To have to be perfect will keep you from going after the dreams you hold so dear.
Letting go of perfection keeps your dreams in sight,
You can enjoy the journey and feel just right.
Letting go of perfection allows you to be wrong.
By being perfectly imperfect, your life can become an inspirational song.

Verse 1

To have to be perfect can result in a heart quake.
To have to be perfect may keep you awake.
Being perfectly imperfect gives you an opportunity to learn.
Being perfectly imperfect keeps you from having a heart burn.
When you have to be perfect without a fault,
Seeking your goals will come to a halt.
When you have to be perfect, you cannot see yourself as you are.
You may rationalize, become defensive, and keep people afar.
Being perfectly imperfect frees you to have unconditional love.
Being perfectly imperfect provides the peace symbolized by a dove.
Being perfect imperfect allows you to have a learning curve.
By having to be perfect, your life may not survive the swerve.
Being perfectly imperfect strengthens the will.

Having to be perfect can make one ill.
Being perfectly imperfect helps one to forgive.
Having to be perfect, one cannot really live.

Chorus

Being perfectly imperfect allows mistakes to become stepping stones.
When someone has to be perfect, you may hear many moans.
Perfectionism is a tyrant that paralyzes with fear.
To have to be perfect will keep you from going after the dreams you hold
so dear.
Letting go perfection keeps your dreams in sight,
You can enjoy the journey and feel just right.
Letting go perfection allows you to be wrong.
By being perfectly imperfect, your life can become an inspirational song.

Verse 2

By being perfectly imperfect, one can thrive.
To have to be perfect, your life can take a dive.
Being perfectly imperfect allows one to be energetic.
Having to be perfect can give you the feeling of being pathetic.
Being perfectly imperfect, you will not be filled with regret.
Having to be perfect keeps you mistakenly stuck as you cannot forget.
Being perfectly imperfect provides a life that excels.
Having to be perfect can be like a prison where one dwells.
Being perfectly imperfect can provide freedom to live in the now.
Having to be perfect prevents a person from knowing how.
Being perfectly imperfect helps one's life to flow.
Being perfectly imperfect keeps you on the go.
By being perfectly imperfect, what wonderful gifts you will bestow.
By being perfectly imperfect, you will stand up to life toe to toe.
In this way, your creative ventures will flow.
By being perfectly imperfect, your eyes will sparkle and your face will glow.

Chorus

Being perfectly imperfect allows mistakes to become stepping stones.
When someone has to perfect, you may hear many moans,
Being perfectly imperfect, you can keep your dreams in sight,
You can enjoy the journey and feel just right.
Letting go perfection allows you to be wrong.
By being perfectly imperfect, your life can become an inspirational song.
By being perfectly imperfect, your life can become an inspirational song.
By being perfectly imperfect, your life can become an inspirational song.

6. Good Habits Prevent Chasing Rabbits
Dan C. Crenshaw

Chorus

Good habits can keep you from chasing after rabbits
Good habits can ward off life's difficult bullets.
Good habits can enhance assists and prevent debits.
By having good habits, you will be empowered to be acknowledged by many credits.
Good habits can enable you to evaluate all facets.
Good habits can help you to be one of the favorites.
Good habits will prevent you from experiencing forfeits.
Good habits can empower you to hit your targets.

Verse 1

Good habits will help you to handle any obstacles and culprits.
With good habits, you will not be a person who nervously fidgets.
Good habits will give you more possibilities and fewer limits.
Good habits will provide you with many merits.
Good habits will bring you many kinds of profits.
Good habits will prevent you from having embarrassing secrets.
Good habits will attract opportunities like magnets.
Good habits can help your life to become more pristine.
Good habits can help you to be more serene.

Good habits can help make your coping muscles more lean.
Good habits can create possibilities in the future that are presently unseen.
Good habits can become like energizing, nutritious protein.
Good habits can help you create a bridge over a life-challenging ravine.

Good habits can keep the bugs out of your life like a windscreen.
Good habits can produce results that have not previously been seen.
With good habits, your mind will be consistently keen.

Chorus

Good habits can keep you from chasing after rabbits
Good habits can ward off life's difficult bullets.
Good habits can enhance assists and prevent debits.
By having good habits, you will be empowered to be acknowledged by many credits.
Good habits can enable you to evaluate all facets.
Good habits can help you to be one of the favorites.
Good habits will prevent you from experiencing forfeits.
Good habits can empower you to hit your targets.

Verse 2

Good habits can help a toxic environment like a shot of vaccine.
Good habits can keep you less stressed as you live in the present moment.
Good habits can help you ward off a possible ailment.
With good habits, you will not be so drained that your talents will not lie dormant.
A good habit can become a stress treatment.
With good habits, encroachments won't feel like your head has just hit the pavement.
With good habits, your life will be more valiant.
Good habits can increase your self-esteem.
Good habits can give you energy for inspiration to fashion a life scheme.
Good habits can make your life efficient and buoyant.
You can see that with focused energy, you can be brilliant.
Regarding reaching purpose, passion, and excellence, you will be content.
With less stress, you are less apt to be errant.

With good habits, you will be much more fervent.
With good habits, procrastination will not be a tyrant.
With good habits, your strengths will be in the forefront.

Chorus

Good habits can keep you from chasing after rabbits
Good habits can ward off life's difficult bullets.
Good habits can enhance assists and prevent debits.
By having good habits, you will be empowered to be acknowledged by many credits.
Good habits can empower you to hit your targets.
Good habits can empower you to hit your targets
Good habits can empower you to hit your targets.
Good habits can empower you to hit your targets.

7. When your Dog is Gone (Expansion of my Poem in the Introduction)
Dan C. Crenshaw

Chorus

Doggone it, my dog is gone.
What went wrong?
Why can I be strong?
I cry all day long.
People tell me tears do not belong.
These words throw salt on my bleeding heart.
It seems that my dog and I were never a part.
I need someone to understand.
The precious dog wagged his tail as I came home again and again.

Verse 1

"It was just a pet," I hear over and over.
He was more than a pet; he was my companion named Rover.
He loved me 100 percent of the time.

His presence gave me a connection seemingly divine.
The look in his eyes let me know his love was mine.
In my mind, I heard melodious bells chime.
We relished each moment in harmony.
He never seemed angry at me.
He helped me to see what kind of person I could be.
My welcome-home experiences will never be the same.
He always was elated when I came.
He danced and pranced in sheer delight.
No matter how the day went, my precious pet made things all right.
How can anyone say that his death was trite?
I loved that dog with all of my heart, soul, and might.
The bond that we had was out of sight.
Regarding life's values, he often helped me to see the light.

Chorus

Doggone it, my dog is gone.
What went wrong?
Why can I be strong?
I cry all day long.
People tell me tears do not belong.
These words throw salt on my bleeding heart.
It seems that my dog and I were never a part.
I need someone to understand.
The precious dog wagged his tail as I came home again and again.

Verse 2

How much I miss him goes beyond any words.
A painful memory constantly occurs.
Every moment we were together, my heart was stirred.
Not taking this loss seriously is more than absurd.
People think I should be completely undeterred.
They cannot see why his loss deserves a word.
They want me to act as if the loss never occurred.
In shock, my mind, body, and spirit are blurred.
They have no idea what my emotions have incurred.

I wish that my pet could have been cured.
The worst that happened is what I feared.
These unprecedented feelings feel uncomfortably weird.
For the pain of this loss, I would never have been fully prepared.
It is as if a trap has caught my heart and it is painfully snared.
I wish that experiencing the death of my pet could have been spared.
It would be nice to be comforted by someone who understood and cared.

Chorus

Doggone it, my dog is gone.
I can see him romping in the fields in heaven waiting for me to come home.
We than can feel each other's spirit as he playfully roams.
Doggone it, my dog is gone.
But I will see him when I go home.
But I will see him when I go home

8. From Grief to Greatness
Dan C. Crenshaw

Chorus

Death brings many hurtful feelings that can be experienced as culprits.
You may long for the day that you will begin to experience emotional summits.
You have the challenge of strengthening your adaptability.
When you endure the journey and cope, you can see your possibility.

Verse 1

Grief can feel very brutal.
Spoken words that do not fit can feel futile.
These words can become noxious to the soul
And allow grief to enable one emotionally and physically to continuously feel old.
One can continually feel emotionally dead.
Facing each day can become a dread

With a recovering attitude, one can gradually become alive instead.
It can gradually enable one to recoil out of bed.
One faces the day with hope and possibilities that are ahead.
It will be nice when memories of your pet seem like pleasant visits.
With valor in dealing with your grief, you can experience coping merits.
People do not want to see grief in its totality.
The anguish of grief is a commonality.
One must face grief with practicality.
Reality can help one to move through grief with creativity.
They will avoid escaping grief through non-reality.
One can grow from grief to greatness by facing reality.

Chorus

Death brings many hurtful feelings that can be experienced as culprits.
You may long for the day that you will begin to experience emotional summits.
You have the challenge of strengthening your adaptability.
When you cope creatively with the grief journey, you can see greater possibility.

Verse 2

The process of grief at its best can feel gruesome.
The challenge is keeping up with the painful journey with courage that is awesome.
Some people may try to steal your grief.
Without the journey through grief, there can be no relief.
A person who strives to take your grief away will hinder your purposeful belief.
People may want to minimize your grief as an insignificant fender bender.
You need someone to understand to help become a caring grief mender.
Many people may attempt to assuage the pain of loss by utilizing triviality.
You can find supportive people that will see the reality of grief's feeling of brutality.
Some unsupportive people may see the level of your pain as abnormality.
The truth is the pain of grief is reality.
Many people are helped by spirituality.

It helps people to accept earthly death's finality.
They creatively cope with reality.
They can come to terms with fatality.
Growing from grief to greatness involves strengthening one's mentality.

Chorus

Death brings many hurtful feelings that can be experienced as culprits.
You may long for the day that you will begin to experience emotional summits.
You have the challenge of strengthening your adaptability.
When you cope creatively with the grief journey, you can see your possibility.

9. Lean into your Dreams
Dan C. Crenshaw

Chorus

Leaning into an uphill run
Makes running much more efficient and fun.
Leaning away from your dreams may result in a rough ride.
Leaning into your dreams helps you to keep your stride.

Verse 1

When you lean forward when someone is talking, you are more alert.
When you lean forward into a dream, your focus will not divert.
Leaning into your dreams can surface a well-planned scheme.
Leaning into your dreams can help the possibility of your dreams to be seen.
Leaning away from your dreams cay lead you astray.
You never will find if there is a possible way.
Your life will be unstable, and you are likely to fall.
It may feel like your dreams have hit a wall.
Leaning forward helps you to assert their most efficient actions.
Leaning backward one can only have hapless reactions.
Leaning forward will serve as a bridge to go over an obstacle.

Leaning backward can result in a debacle.
When you lean forward when someone is talking, you are more alert.
When you lean forward into a dream, your focus will not divert.
Leaning into your dreams can surface a well-planned scheme.
Leaning into your dreams can help the possibility of your dreams to be seen.

Chorus

Leaning into an uphill run
Makes running much more efficient and fun.
Leaning away from your dreams may result in a rough ride.
Leaning into your dreams helps you to keep your stride.

Verse 2

When you lean away from your dreams, they do not come to reality.
The final destination of the dream can feel like fatality.
Leaning into your dreams can inspire others to follow.
When you lean away from your dreams, you can only wallow.
Inspiring others to follow you can provide much more momentum.
People working together toward a dream can prevent a conundrum.
The eye of the hurricane is calm.
When you lean into life, your creativity can become a healing balm.
When you lean forward when someone is talking, you are more alert.
When you lean forward into a dream, your focus will not divert.
Leaning into your dreams can surface a well-planned scheme.
Leaning into your dreams can help the possibility of your dreams to be seen.
When you lean backward, opportunities can pass you by.
Not being in a position take the opportunity could make you cry.
By leaning forward, one can seize the moment.
Then opportunities can be taken, warding off torment.

Chorus

Leaning into your dreams can surface a well-planned scheme.
Leaning into your dreams can enable your dreams to be seen.
Leaning into your dreams can enable your dreams to be seen.
Leaning into your dreams can enable your dreams to be seen.

10. Taming Shame
Dan C. Crenshaw

Chorus

When shame is tamed, one can bring treasure out of what feels like trash.
One's self-esteem can become free of shame and bring emotional cash.
Pain will then have a different texture and will not bash.
One can gradually heal as shame stops lashing the wounds.
Then coming to terms with shame will not take endless moons.
The eclipse of the sun will be over.
The shining light will set one free from darkness's dreadful cover.
The bright light will put shame to shame and spark one to recover.

Verse 1

When guilt becomes infected and worsens, it can turn into shame.
If guilt or false guilt is not released, it can brutally maim.
Taming the shaming malaise is difficult to obtain.
It is deep feelings of being worthless with no value to gain.
Shame chews up one's self-esteem and spits it out.
Then one's esteem is in shock and cannot scream and shout.
Sometimes one can get stuck in shame, which is guilt gone wild.
A person may be shame-based from being abused as a child.
People who have a shame-based personality may have a particular challenge
in gaining peace.
This shame may make it difficult feelings of false or real guilt to release.
Negative feelings can grow deeper as the power of shame can amaze.
Shame then sets one's heart ablaze.

To be shame-based can create developmental delays, as shame can place one's mind in a daze.
To experience shame can be more than a phase.
Life can become a complex, confusing maze.
Mistakes can continue replays, and a person can stay in an emotional malaise.
Shame can be an emotion that betrays.

Chorus

When the shame is tamed, then it can be harnessed.
With the controlling bit in shame's mouth,
One will no longer feel bitten with one's life going south.
One can bring treasure out of what feels like trash.
One's self-esteem can become free of shame and bring emotional cash.
Pain then will have a different texture and will not bash.
One can gradually heal, as shame stops lashing the wounds.
Then coming to terms with grief will not take endless moons.
The eclipse of the sun will be over.
The shining light will set one free from darkness's dreadful cover.
The bright light will put shame to shame and spark one to recover.

Verse 2

False humiliation can result in an attitudinal, damaging mutilation.
This aspect of shame can result in negative rumination that resists cessation.
A continual feeling of shame can result in one's life's stagnation.
As you mercilessly continue false self-accusation,
You may lose your compass and wisdom in your life's navigation.
As a result, it may prolong you from reaching your destination of restoration.
You may feel that you have not made a mistake.
You may feel that you are a mistake.
Then you may come to the conclusion that there are no redeeming virtues to make.
Living in the darkness of shame is taking the total weight of needless blame.
Shame then can result in one feeling lame.
Shame's teeth can bite and deeply maim.
The winds of shame can result in life feeling more blustery.

Shame can make grief seem scary.
To feel false guilt can make you feel more queasy and shaky.
Shame can make grief feel like an even greater calamity
And as a result, you can feel sulky.

Chorus

When the shame is tamed then it can be harnessed.
With the controlling bit in shame's mouth,
One will no longer feel bitten with one's life going south.
One can bring treasure out of what feels like trash.
One's self-esteem can become free of shame and bring emotional cash.
Pain then will have a different texture and will not bash.
The eclipse of the sun will be over.
The shining light will set one free from darkness's dreadful cover.
The bright light will put shame to shame and spark one to recover.

Verse 3

You may feel demeaned and then have an attitude toward yourself that is mean.
Who you really are is not what it may seem.
Guilt can be good in helping you to grow toward being a better person.
You can learn from your poor choices and move away from evil.
Your mistakes can become stepping stones.
On the other hand, shame can put you on a downward slide.
You may experience healing as you have cried.
Shame is a distorting dynamic that always lies.
The feelings of shame can come from abuse and trauma.
It can prick and perpetuate the pain of a past, tragic drama.
This sense of disgrace preoccupies one by exaggerating one's limitations.
A sense of worthlessness can blind one to one's possibilities.
Shame negates the reality that we are priceless.
Shame can infect the mind, body, and soul and become relentless.
You can gradually heal as shame stops lashing your wounds.
Then coming to terms with shame will not take endless moons.

Chorus

When the shame is tamed then it can be harnessed.
With the controlling bit in shame's mouth,
You will no longer feel bitten with your life going south.
You can bring treasure out of what feels like trash.
Your self-esteem can become free of shame and bring emotional cash.
Pain then will have a different texture and will not bash.
The eclipse of the sun will be over.
The shining light will set you free from darkness's dreadful cover.
The bright light will put shame to shame and spark you to recover.

11. It Is Mean Not to Give Life Meaning
Dan C. Crenshaw

Chorus

It is mean not to give life meaning.
Without meaning, your mind may begin screaming.
Becoming a cynic can leave your emotions screeching.
If a cynic has goals, they are meaningless and far-reaching.
A cynic does not want to find meaning.
It is mean to you and to the world to not find some purpose.
Bringing meaning evokes purpose within
And gives out positive energy to inspire others to purposefully begin.

Verse 1

What is happening may give no answer and could be mysterious.
Instead of interpreting life with meaning, you may say life is preposterous.
At times, your purpose may not seem clear.
Some difficult events seem senseless when they appear.
Meaning can help one to live with the questions when there are no answers.
If you have no purpose for your life, it is like your emotions filled with cancers.
Your behavior will seem like a treadmill going nowhere.
You will not have strong willpower that can get you meaningfully there.
You may have a chronic expression that scours.

That expression can create a life that sours.

It can wilt the beauty of flowers.

It can hide the sunlight and bring out meaningless and never-ending fright.

People's search for meaning is personal and unique.

This meaningful and purposeful search can provide a positive lifestyle technique.

Then the journey will give you meaning as you move toward the destiny you seek.

It is mean not to make like meaningful.

Your behavior, thoughts, and feelings mean that you are making life purposeful.

Chorus

It is mean not to give life meaning.

Without meaning, your mind may begin screaming.

Becoming a cynic can leave your emotions screeching.

If a cynic has goals, they are meaningless and scarcely reaching.

A cynic does not want to find meaning.

A cynic is mean to you and to the world and can be demeaning.

Bringing meaning evokes a purpose within.

And gives out positive energy that inspires others to purposefully begin.

Verse 2

Living on purpose has a specific intention.

Living on purpose brings priorities to one's attention.

To have purpose is to have a vision and a mission.

To live with yourself as you encounter challenges, you can be just.

With a healthy sense of self, you will rebound and not feel disgust.

Purpose brings fulfillment to the mind, body, and soul.

Without a purpose, we are walking in the dark.

We react to what is happening and become a ship without a rudder.

When we realize what we have done, we may shudder.

When we react instead of act, it may result in a destructive blunder.

When we react instead of act, we may end up asunder.

When we act intentionally, we can become an ambassador.

When we react instead of act regarding our actions, we may become puzzled and wonder.
When we react instead of act regarding our goals, we may blunder.
When we react instead of act in relationships, we may become an intruder.
When we react instead of act, we may have to run for cover.

Chorus

It is mean not to give life meaning.
Without meaning, your mind may begin screaming.
Bringing meaning evokes a purpose within
And gives out positive energy to inspire others to purposefully begin.
Becoming a cynic can leave your emotions screeching.
If a cynic has goals, they are meaningless and scarcely reaching.
A cynic does not want to find meaning.
It is mean to you and to the world to not find some purpose.

Verse 3

We need purpose to cut on the lights to see where we need to go.
Then we will not be like a ship that is tossed to and fro.
A lighthouse will guide the ship safely to shore.
The ship will ship out cynicism and grant purposes galore.
Purpose spawns creativity and options to increase meaning more.
Purpose can occur when you console a friend whose heart is sore
What gives you purpose is what stirs your passion about living.
What brings you purpose is what motivates excellence in your living.
Motivation can increase when we see the purpose's ultimate impact.
This empowerment will undergird hope and keep it intact.
Having a purpose can keep a person's behavior on track.
Having a passionate purpose can lead to breakthroughs.
Your thoughts, feelings, and actions can overcome obstacles that renew.
To have a purpose helps you to find creative, workable solutions.
Then you can be committed to your purpose's devotions.
Your life will not be filled with meaningless motions.
With purpose, you will use your head for ideas that are aloft.
Then the direction will become clear that you have sought.

Chorus

It is mean not to give life meaning.
Some people try to make meaning out of scheming.
Someone with a strong purpose has focus in their eyes.
Their life is authentic and is not filled with lies.
They live in the present moment with meaning that prevents frustrating sighs.
Their clarity of purpose can bring a sparkle to their eyes.
Their clarity of purpose can bring a sparkle to their eyes.
Their clarity of purpose can bring a sparkle to their eyes.

12. Prevent Messing with Stressing
Dan C. Crenshaw

Chorus

Prevent messing with stressing.
Your serene life can become a blessing.
Stress can dampen your life with strife.
Serenity can breathe within you the breath of life.

Verse 1

Prevent messing with stressing.
Calming thoughts can help your mind to begin resting.
Contemplate a fresh stream
Reflecting the rays of a sunbeam.
Envision being splashed all over by a waterfall,
Breathtakingly giving you a comforting shawl.
Envision a rose garden in full bloom.
You will be relaxed very soon.
Every color of roses that you can imagine is there.
You are engulfed by roses that are everywhere.
The sweet smell of roses radiates a savoring scent.
You are enraptured as your five senses are without a dent
Envision a meadow full of beautiful flowers.
And how you would feel lying there for hours.

Envision a smooth lake with no wind
And sitting on a bench relaxing with a close friend.

Chorus

Prevent messing with stressing.
Your serene life can become a blessing.
Stress can dampen your life with strife.
Serenity can breathe within you the breath of life.

Verse 2

Prevent messing with stressing.
Not feeling the thorns on the rose is a serene blessing.
To be serene is to be like a ship coming to its harbor to dock.
To be serene is to be like a character that is solid as a rock.
To be serene is to be like a bird gliding with the wind.
To be serene is to gaze as the blue ocean that has no end.
To be serene is to be like a bird chirping at the top of a tree.
To be serene is to be like finding a lost key.
To be serene is to be like a kite sailing high in the sky.
To be serene is to be like a golden sunset in your mind's eye.
Envision a mountain that is majestic and strong
With a calm lake reflecting its beauty all day long.
To be serene is like a sparkling new ship set free at sea.
To be serene is to be like a soul experiencing eternity.
Preventing messing with stressing has made you extraordinarily serene.
You have gained what serenity can truly mean.

Chorus

Prevent messing with stressing.
Your serene life can become a blessing.
Stress can dampen your life with strife.
Serenity can breathe within you the breath of life.
Stress can dampen your life with strife.
Serenity can breathe within you the breath of life.
Stress can dampen your life with strife.
Serenity can breathe within you the breath of life.

CONCLUSION

It takes much energy to move through grief to greatness
It is significant to recognize your energy
drainers as well as energy gainers.

When your energy drainers
Go down the drain,
You can become transformed
And never be the same.

You can focus on your mission,
With a sound personal vision.
Your energy gainers can produce a life of relevance
And pursue, purpose, passion and excellence.

The journey from grief to greatness
Does not bring arrogance.
It is a journey of self-devotion
And deep reverence.

—Dan Crenshaw

Energy Drainers

Ponder these questions to help clarify your energy drainers:

What parts of your life are going least well?
What are your energy drainers in your work?
What are your energy drainers in your family?

What are your energy drainers in finances?
What are your energy drainers from present life circumstances in general?
What are your energy drainers from your physical health?
What are your energy drainers in dealing with difficult people?
What do you need to let go in attitudes and behavior?

Energy Gainers

Ponder these questions to help clarify your energy gainers:

What makes you feel the most alive and invigorated?
What are your passions in life?
What brings you purpose in life?
What is life calling you to do now?
What would you like to change in your life?
What are your priorities?
Are there things you feel you cannot change that possibly could be changeable?
What do you need to let go?
What are strengths that you can develop further?

Empowerment and focused serene concentration comes from accepting what you cannot change
with serenity and changing what you can with courage and having the wisdom to distinguish the one from the other.

As you move from grief to greatness it is more motivational to build from your strengths.
To be able to mobilize your strengths and make peace when you feel weak.

Remember: *Your life's efforts have not gone for naught*
Commended yourself for what you have already wrought
You are not starting from scratch
You have long since been hatched.

1.   What unchangeable aspects of life do you need to accept and let go?
For example, making peace with what you cannot change can be foundational for you use your strengths to move from grief to greatness.

It is very difficult to let go the unalterable aspects of life.
Coming to terms with what you cannot change can reduce internal strife.
Then becoming serenely focused can lead to a more fulfilling life.
You can make a difference that counts.
And the misguided behaviors you can renounce.

2. What are some things you that you may be striving to change in the wrong manner?

Does the end justify the means?
Is the process worthy of the progress?
Does the manner of change have good manners?

It can help by thinking of an example of what you have changed in a positive manner and begin from a positive feeling.

When you change things in the wrong way there is no serenity.
There will likely only be enmity.
The end will not justify the means which may just feel mean.

3. What are you striving to change that you should not be trying to alter?

Trying to make improvements may be in the best of intentions,
But these efforts going awry can result in futile dissentions.

4. What do you need to change behaviorally regarding the full scope of my life?

You need to affirm what you are doing well.
Owning these strengths can help you feel swell.
You can then take the next step with inspiration.
Then the next step of growth will not be out of desperation.
One can begin to row with the flow
And experience life's progressive journey with a glow.

5.   What do you need to change regarding your feelings/attitudes concerning the complete ramifications of your life?

One's attitude is one's life's outlook.
If it is negative it can lead to a donnybrook.
If one's outlook is positive it can provide one a life's stance,
To celebrate each day with the feelings of wanting to dance.

From the Author

When your dog is gone
May you experience creative furry farewell support
As your creative grief-coping skills increase and your symptoms abort.
May you grow from grief to greatness
As your passion grows and overcomes any apprehensiveness.

—Dan Crenshaw

For further assistance you can have a free 30 minute consultation from me to explore if you would like coaching assistance.

My email address is <u>danc0294@gmail.com</u> and my cell number is 623-293-8087. Questions will be responded to as well.

Printed in the United States
By Bookmasters